# AMERICAN WOMEN
## images and realities

# AMERICAN WOMEN
Images and Realities

*Advisory Editors*
ANNETTE K. BAXTER
LEON STEIN

*A Note About This Volume*

In her long life, Julia Ward Howe (1819-1910) ultimately became the "dearest old lady in America" whose frequent platform appearances were inevitably greeted with her "Battle Hymn of the Republic." She endured a difficult marriage, had five children, and wrote poetry. But a love of causes and a talent for organizing made her founder and prime mover of numerous suffrage, relief and peace organizations. When Dr. Edward Clarke's *Sex in Education* argued that higher education destroyed the physique and psyche of females, she rallied the contributors to this book, whose own lives provided refutation.

# Sex *and* Education

## 𝕬 𝕽𝖊𝖕𝖑𝖞

TO

## DR. E. H. CLARKE'S "SEX IN EDUCATION."

### Julia Ward Howe, *editor*

ARNO PRESS

A New York Times Company
New York • 1972

Reprint Edition 1972 by Arno Press Inc.

American Women:  Images and Realities
ISBN for complete set: 0-405-04445-3
See last pages of this volume for titles.

Manufactured in the United States of America

- - - - - - - - - - ÷ - -

**Library of Congress Cataloging in Publication Data**

Howe, Julia (Ward) 1819-1910, ed.
    Sex and education:  *see  slip*

    (American women:  images and realities)
    Reprint of the 1874 ed.
    1.  Clarke, Edward Hammond, 1820-1877.  Sex in edu-
cation.  2.  Education of women.  3.  Women--Health and
hygiene.  I.  Title.  II.  Series.
LC1621.C7H8  1972          376          72-2608
ISBN 0-405-04463-1

# Sex *and* Education.

## A Reply

TO

## DR. E. H. CLARKE'S "SEX IN EDUCATION."

EDITED, WITH AN INTRODUCTION,

By MRS. JULIA WARD HOWE.

QUI LEGIT REGIT

BOSTON:

ROBERTS BROTHERS.

1874.

*Cambridge:*
*Press of John Wilson and Son.*

# CONTENTS.

———◆———

# INTRODUCTION.

----

I DO not know that I can better introduce this volume than by saying that it contains the views of a number of thoughtful persons, chiefly women, upon the matters treated of in Dr. EDWARD H. CLARKE's work entitled "Sex in Education," and upon the book itself. Nearly all the papers here presented were contributed to various publications soon after the appearance of that book; several of them have been revised by their authors. Each is an independent expression of opinion, modified by no plan or intention of subsequent combination. The general agreement in their tenor, and the permission to republish them at this time and in this form, afford the only ground upon which the Editor can assume to speak for their authors. Her "we" therefore must be taken with this limitation.

Most of the writers are experienced in the office of tuition, and in the observation of its effects. All of them have had occasion to form their own theories of what is desirable for the improvement of the condition of women. The facts and experience of their lives have led them far from Dr. Clarke's conclusions. To most of them, his book seems to have found a chance *at* the girls, rather than a chance *for* them. All could wish that he had not played his sex-symphony so harshly, so loudly, or in so public a manner. But since he has awakened public attention with his discovered discord, all would gladly combine in reassuring mankind of the compatibility of its foremost interests. Dr. Clarke's discord exists not in nature, but in his own thought. An appeal to the great laws of harmony will be sure to solve it, and set it out of sight.

Most of us feel compelled to characterize this book in one aspect as an intrusion into the sacred domain of womanly privacy. No woman could publish facts and speculations concerning the special physical economy of the other sex, on so free and careless a plane, without incurring the gravest rebuke for insolence and immodesty. And yet it is important that mothers should know enough of these to guide and influence their sons in the right direction. But no man could endure the thought of having the physical functions peculiar to his sex so unveiled before the common sight of society, so suggested to and imposed upon its common talk. However, then, people may differ concerning the coarseness or refinement of the book, all must, we think, agree that its method violates the Christian rule of doing to others exactly as we would have them do to us.

Despite Dr. Clarke's prominent position in this community, we do not feel compelled to regard him as the supreme authority on the subjects of which he treats. The object, then, of our publication is twofold. First and foremost we wish to put in a solid and tangible form the impression which his book makes upon men and women to whom the interests of Woman and of Humanity have long been the theme of careful study and anxious thought. And in the second place we desire to appeal to the wisdom and chivalry of the two professions on whose blended domain the book imposes its forced and absolute conclusions.

To those most eminent in physics and in sociology we would say: " Take the social mixture of to-day, with its antecedents and concomitants. Analyze it fairly and thoroughly; and then tell us if the over-education of women is its most poisonous ingredient."

To the high courts of education we would say: "Remodel carefully your laws and ordinances. The mischiefs arising from the separation of the sexes during the period of education are such as to make their co-education imperative. Youth cannot be driven and overworked in one sex with more impunity than in the other. Boys as well as girls break down under severe study, men as well as women, and at least as often. Let a milder and more humane *régime* be devised and enforced. No one loses health through the lessons of wisdom wisely explained. It is the hurried, undigested (also indigestible) tuition which nauseates and fatigues. Let the community be careful not only of what is taught, but of how it is taught. And above all, in view of the good of society, let not man and woman, who are to be partners in all the earnest tasks of life, come forth from a separate and unequal disci-

1*

pline, to meet as strangers in their fiery youth. What knowledge of character, what insight into sympathy and compatibility, may we not hope to find among young people who have met in the august presence of wisdom and science; who have assisted each other, not in the mazes of a bewildering dance, but in noble operations of intellect, in unravelling the problems of the ages, in building the structure of the social world!"

And to parents may we not say: Do not longer feel obliged to surrender your daughters, in the very bloom of their youthful powers, to the unintelligent dominion of Fashion. You subject them to the extravagant, immodest rules of display; you expose them to the intercourse of flattery and folly, to the poison of heated and crowded rooms, late hours, and luxurious suppers. You countenance the lavish waste of time, talent, sensibility, and money, and all this because without it your daughters may not marry. And with it, indeed, they may not. Take courage then, and come to a loftier stand. Educate the future wives with the future husbands. Give the two in common the highest enjoyments and the happiest memories. Then shall the marriage wreath crown the pair in its true human dignity, never to be displaced or lost.

J. W. H.

# SEX AND EDUCATION.

---

## I.

### BY JULIA WARD HOWE.

WHEN a book challenges public attention to its especial object and intention, we may not inappropriately deal with it before we consider its author. As to the book, then, called "Sex in Education," let us endeavor to make up our minds concerning its character, before we pass on to deal with the topics it suggests.

Is the book, then, a work of science, of literature, or of philosophy, or is it a simple practical treatise on the care of health ? We should call it none of these. It has neither the impartiality of science, the form of literature, the breadth of philosophy, nor the friendliness of counsel.

It is a work of the polemic type, presenting a persistent and passionate plea against the admission of women to a collegiate education in common with men. The advisableness of such education in common is a question upon which people differ greatly in opinion. So many people of conscience and intelligence hold opposite theories concerning this, that it may be considered as a question fairly open to discussion, and asking to be tested in the light of experience. Dr. Clarke supports his side of the argument by a statement of facts insufficient for his purpose, and by reasonings and inferences irrelevant to the true lesson of these facts. He makes in the first place a strange confusion between things present, past, and future, and in the terror of the identical education to come sees identical education of the sexes in the past and present as the cause of all the ills that female flesh is heir to. He asserts the fact of an ascertained and ever increasing deterioration in the persons of American women from the true womanly standard. He finds them tending ever more

and more towards a monstrous type, sterile and
sexless ; and these facts, which some of us may
strongly doubt, he considers accounted for by
the corresponding fact that boys and girls receive the same intellectual education. According to him, you cannot feed a woman's brain
without starving her body. Brain and body are
set in antagonism over against each other, and
what is one organ's meat is another's poison.
Single women of the intellectual type he char-
acterizes very generally, not only as *agamai*,
but as *agenes ;* and his portraiture of them is
sufficiently revolting. The powerful influence
of climate is lightly estimated by him. One
hundred years would be insufficient to change
the stout, heavily boned English or Irish woman,
with her abundant covering of flesh, into the
wiry, nervous Yankee woman, characterized by
nerve and brain. The cause of all this, of the
undeveloped busts, fragile figures, and uncer-
tain health of American women, resides in the
fact that with us, as he says, girls and boys
receive the same education.

The periodical function peculiar to women is a point upon which Dr. Clarke dwells with persistent iteration. Its neglect he considers the principal source of disease among the women of our land. Its repression or over-production are equally fatal to health ; and, in the years which nature consecrates to its establishment, the recurrence of the function should be observed by the avoidance of bodily and mental fatigue. Dr. Clarke's reasoning upon this point affirms that American women neglect care in this direction beyond all other women, and that the school education which our girls receive is the moving cause of this neglect.

We cannot remember a single point in Dr. Clarke's diagnosis of American female hygiene which is not included in the present rapid *résumé.* The Doctor's prognosis is even more dismal and unpromising. Open the doors of your colleges to women, and you will accomplish the ruin of the Commonwealth. Disease — already, according to him, the rule among them — will become without exception. Your girls will lose their physical stature, and your boys their mental stature, since the tasks set for the latter would be limited by the periodical disability of the girls. The result will be a physical and sexual chaos, out of which the Doctor sees no escape save in an act akin to the rape of the Sabines. Tennyson's line suits with his mood : —

> "I will take some savage woman, she shall rear my dusky
> race."

A number of persons have commented wisely and wittily upon this book and its contents. There is, perhaps, no need of any further detailed criticism of its scope and statement. We have endeavored to give its sense and spirit in little. And we will supplement this synopsis by giving as briefly our own impressions concerning these.

To begin with the observance of the periodical function. This is a good old grandmotherly doctrine, handed down from parent to child through all the ages of humanity. Ignorance of the laws of health would, no doubt, in all

ages, induce young persons to disregard the
cautions of their elders on this as on other
points ; and the sharp proverb which tells what
young people think of old people, and what the
latter know of the former, must often recur to
the minds of elderly women preaching care and
prudence to daughters and nieces.   On the
whole, if a pretty wide and long personal experience can go for any thing, I incline to think
that the elder generation is much more careful
of this point of health than of any other.   Many
young women who are allowed to eat, dress, live,
and behave as they like, are periodically kept
from all violent exercise and fatigue, so far as
the vigilance of elders can accomplish this.   The
wilfulness and ingenuity of the young, however,
are often more than a match for this vigilance ;
and a single ride on horseback, a single wetting
of the feet, or indulgence in the irresistible
German, may entail lifelong misery, which the
maternal or friendly guardian has done all in
her power to prevent.   I myself once knew a
German lady who, married and childless for

many years, confessed to me that a ball attended in her early youth was the cause of this misfortune.

I have known of repeated instances of incurable disease and even of death arising from rides on horseback taken at the critical period. I have known fatal pulmonary consumption to arise from exposure of the feet in silk stockings, at winter parties. Every matron knows and relates these sad facts to the young girls under her charge. They are sometimes heeded, oftener not. Nothing in our knowledge of youth would lead us to consider them as of rare occurrence. And yet Dr. Clarke attributes most failures of the function and its concomitant, maternity, to the school education received by our girls.

The accusation then of systematic neglect of the periodic function by the educators of youth among us cannot be admitted without more evidence than Dr. Clarke has thus far given us. That women in America particularly neglect their health, that women violate the laws of their constitution as men cannot violate theirs, and that the love of intellectual pursuits causes them to do so, — this is the fable out of which Dr. Clarke draws the moral that women must not go to college with men. Fable and moral appear equally unsubstantial. If Dr. Clarke had said that the best men and women of the State, the wisest and noblest, should never allow this subject of education to pass out of their minds or out of their care ; if he had said that, after worthily receiving education, the first duty of man and woman is to secure it to the succeeding generation, he would have pointed to the true remedy for all that is amiss on this head. The great increase in the study of physiology among us, and especially among women, must tend, we are sure, to a wiser and better self-culture and care of the young. Education is necessarily "line upon line and precept upon precept." The elder generation can only do its best, and trust to the docility and good faith of the young.

The special character of Dr. Clarke's book provokes the question whether he has not unduly specialized facts which are general, and not limited to any- coincidence with that which he especially attacks, — the education of American women, and their physique as affected by it. Is it wholly or principally in America that young women fail of sexual development, have imperfect busts, are afflicted with ill-health and insanity, and in marriage are sterile, or if they have children cannot nurse them ?

A well-known sentence of Solomon's shows that even in his time the female form sometimes failed of completeness. Rousseau says of one of the women whom he admired, "*et de la gorge comme de ma main*," with a general slur upon all women so formed. In Paris has been invented and advertised an artificial bosom warranted to palpitate for a whole evening. It is not likely that this invention has been patented for the exclusive use of American women.

To return to Biblical times, one of the persons healed by our Saviour was a woman suffering from what Dr. Clarke would call *menorrhœa.* It may be as well to remark by the way that during the twelve years of her suffering she had spent all that she had upon physicians, and still was nothing the better, but rather the worse. Sterility was common in the times both of the Old and of the New Testament. It is common to-day among the savages of Africa. It is by no means true that the women who themselves show the greatest physical development are always those whose offspring are the most numerous and healthy. Slender women are often more successful mothers and nurses than the stout sisters whose full outlines attest their own robusticity. Even as to the facts of nursing, women with small breasts often have an abundant supply of milk ; while women with fuller outward development often have little or none.

Andrew Combe in his book on Infancy speaks of the great number of infants who in Germany are brought up by hand. He gives most careful rules for rearing infants on artificial food, and does not treat this as at all an uncommon necessity. English women confined in Italy and other foreign countries proverbially lose their milk, and the profession of wet-nurse to an English family has long been one of the most common in Rome and Naples. Many German women in America are obliged to feed their infants wholly or in part, and many American women are good nurses and prolific mothers.

Again we see in Paris papers advertisements of the new remedies, "which the patient herself can apply, and which will spare her the unpleasant necessity of examinations," &c. Physicians of large practice and experience are able, in all parts of the world, to chronicle many cases of uterine disease, of functional derangement, and of arrested development among women, in which cases no plea of excessive cerebral action induced by over-study is at all admissible. But Dr. Clarke sees disease chiefly in American women. In them reside leucorrhœa, dysmenorrhœa, amenorrhœa, &c. In them are *ateknia, agalactia, amazia*. And the reason why they have all these evils is simply this, some of them wish to enter Harvard College, and some of them have already passed through other colleges.

Now that the topics of sex and education need careful study and remodelling of ideas and methods, nobody is less disposed to deny than the writer of these lines. She is perfectly sure that the philosophy of sex is thus far little understood in America, or anywhere else. She has the same impression concerning the philosophy of education. The physical evils attendant upon the female constitution are as old as that constitution itself. They deserve and require the most careful investigation. But the feminine hygiene will be higher and more complete when it is administered by women. Personal experience adds an important element even to the closest and most scientific observation.

Before this pet theory of the incompatibility of health with intellectual activity, for women only, was discovered, men of science speculated concerning the deficient busts of American

women. The dry, stimulating climate was sup-
posed, in a great measure, to account for it.
The fact itself reaches back to the grandmothers
of the grandmothers of to-day. It was and is
chiefly observable in the northern and eastern
States. As you go south, you find fuller forms,
but not always combined with emptier heads.
The effect of the climate of this portion of the
country upon the masculine physique is equally
noticeable, and has long been a subject of remark. Men here are for the most part wiry,
sinewy, nervous, and brainy. If any of us, carrying out Dr. Clarke's views, prefer to mate
with men in whom flesh and muscle counter-
poise the tyrannous nerve system, we too must
go over the borders, and bring the progenitors
of the future race from lands where the east
wind blows not. But this reminds us of the
well-known overplus of sixty thousand single
women in Massachusetts alone. Dr. Clarke
arraigns the mothers, actual and possible, for
being no better than they are. But what is he
going to do about the impossible fathers, in view

of the coming generation to which he is so devoted ?

If one thing could be more astonishing than another in Dr. Clarke's treatment of his subject, we should give the palm to his consideration of the influence of climate on the human organism. He is unwilling to consider it at all as a factor in the alleged ill-health of American women. According to him one hundred years are not enough to mould the European organism in accordance with the American type. If this is really his opinion, his experience must have differed widely from that of others. I have observed important effects of modification produced by climate, in shorter periods of time than this. Two brothers of one family, resident in Boston, separated at the conclusion of the Revolutionary War. One remained in this city, one migrated to Nova Scotia. Those who at a later day were able to compare the children of these two gentlemen found the Boston family marked with every characteristic of the New England race, thin, nervous, wiry, alert, intense.

The Nova Scotian family were stout, full-blooded, and plethoric, altogether of the English colonial type.

English families resident in India soon lose the freshness of their coloring and the fulness of their outline. In fact, the adaptation of one nationality to another is sometimes astonishingly rapid. Mr. Burlingame looked almost like a Chinaman before he died. The writer has seen an American official long resident in Turkey whose physiognomy had become entirely that of his adopted country. The potent American climate works quickly in assimilating the foreign material offered to it. Two generations suffice to efface the salient marks of Celtic, Saxon, French, or Italian descent. The Negro alone is able to offer a respectable resistance.

It may occur to some that the assumed identity of the intellectual education given to girls and boys in America may have less to do with the ill-health of the former than the dissimilarity of their physical training. Boys are much in the open air. Girls are much in the house. Boys wear a dress which follows and allows their natural movements. Girls wear clothes which impede and almost paralyze their limbs. Boys have, moreover, the healthful hope held out to them of being able to pursue their own objects, and to choose and follow the business or profession of their choice. Girls have the dispiriting prospect of a secondary and derivative existence, with only so much room allowed them as may not cramp the full sweep of the other sex. The circumstances first named directly affect health, the last exerts a strong reflex action upon it. "We are only women, and it does not matter," passes from mother to daughter. A very estimable young lady said to me the other day, in answer to a plea for dress-reform, "It is better to look handsome, even if it does shorten life a little." Her care of herself probably does not go beyond that indicated by this saying. Dr. Clarke cites a few instances of functional derangement. But by far the most frequent difficulty with our women arises from uterine displacement, and this in turn comes partly from the utter disuse of the muscles which should keep the uterus in place, but which are kept inactive by the corset, weighed upon by the heavy skirt, and drawn upon by the violent and unnatural motion of the dancing at present in vogue. Is it any wonder that these ill-educated, over-burthened muscles give way, like other ill-trained, over-powered things ? Some instances of remarkable robustness in women have been the result of a physical education identical with that usually given to boys. In these cases, the parents, after repeated losses of children through much cherishing, have at last determined to give the girls a chance through athletic sports and unrestricted exercise in the open air. And this has again and again proved successful.

Much in Dr. Clarke's treatment of his subject is objectionable. We are left in doubt whether his book was written for men or for women, and we conclude that his method of statement is not good for either. Much of his remarking upon sex is justly offensive, and his statements concerning those single women of culture whom

he terms *agenes* would scarcely be endured in
any household in which these single saints bear
the burthens of all the others, and lead lives
divinely wedded to duty.   The odious expression which completes his picture of " the girls
tied to their dictionaries," &c., would exclude the
book, and the writer too, from some pure and
polite circles.   And we must say to him, with all
due regard for the good intentions with which
we desire to credit him, —

" These things must not be thought of on this
wise."

I have thus attempted a brief addition to the
comments of women upon Dr. Clarke's work,
telling pretty plainly what I think of it, and why.
But a full discussion of these great themes of
Sex and Education can hardly be had in answer
to a summons so sharp and so partial as his own.
Not to dogmatize and counter-dogmatize upon
these points will make either men or women
wiser.   Not for those who think they know every
thing about the matter to discourse to those
whom they judge as knowing nothing about it.

These processes will always retard instead of advancing the discovery of truth. But when men and women may meet together for fair and equal interchange of thought, the men not wanting in modesty, nor the women in courage, then we shall be glad to listen, if we do not speak. And if we do speak, we shall say, "Father, thou hast made all things well, and without thy wisdom was not any thing made that was made."

## II.

### BY THOS. WENTWORTH HIGGINSON.

THOSE who are anxiously studying the problem of the Education of Women may be trusted to read with eager interest this little book by Dr. Clarke. The author takes pains to recognize the intellectual ability of women ; and he puts on record a most valuable and emphatic denial, from his own professional experience, of the common assertion that American women habitually desire to escape the duties of wifehood and motherhood. I should not call the book generally coarse, but very needlessly rough and plain-spoken, especially for a book destined to popular perusal ; and the author certainly touches the verge of coarseness in his description of a possible sexless woman. He, however, indulges in no unfair fling against the advocates of the equality of the sexes, except as far as is con-

tained in the following sentences: " Woman
seems to be looking up to man and his development, as the goal and ideal of womanhood. The
new gospel of female development glorifies what
she possesses in common with him, and tramples
under her feet as a source of weakness and badge
of inferiority the mechanism and functions peculiar to herself." (p. 129.)   If this is intended to
describe the " gospel " proclaimed by the " Woman's Journal," for instance, there is not a number of the paper, from the beginning, which does
not contain the material wherewith to refute the
statement.   And that it is not true of the agita-
tion in America, as a whole, is shown by the fact
that this movement has been constantly under
criticism from European and Roman Catholic
sources, for precisely the opposite tendency ;
that is, for encouraging the study of physiology
in schools, and for thus making young girls too
well acquainted with those special laws of their
own being, about which they were once studi-
ously kept in ignorance.   The two charges destroy each other: both cannot be true, and I

inferences, whose demands are hardly met by the book now under discussion.

Let us consider, first, Dr. Clarke's facts, and then his inferences.

## I. *Dr. Clarke's Facts.*

I certainly am conscious of no manner of bias against Dr. Clarke, who was my townsman and college classmate ; and I opened his pages, honestly hoping to find an array of facts that should be impressive both by their quality and by their quantity. To show, by citing individual instances, that the pressure of our school system injures health very often, is not enough. To take seven cases out of a physician's note-book, and then assure us that there are a good many more, is not enough. Yet this is precisely what Dr. Clarke does ; and, strange to say, one of these is the case of an actress and another of a clerk, leaving only five educational instances in all. This does not seem to me what would be called, in any other branch of science, a satisfactory basis of facts. For in-

stance, I open the last "American Naturalist,"
and find Professor Wilder thus criticising the
new work on "The Cerebral Convolutions
of Man," by Ecker : "The value of such a gen-
eralization might be estimated if the author
had given us the number of individuals upon
which it is based." This is precisely the criticism I should make on the generalizations of
Dr. Clarke.

That our educational system is faulty on the
physiological side is an old story. The evil
has been under discussion, in a general way,
for years, — by Horace Mann, Dr. Howe, Dr.
Butler of Providence, and by myself, among
others, in a paper called "The Murder of the
Innocents," published in the "Atlantic Monthly" for September, 1859, and afterward included
in "Out Door Papers." It seems to me that
what is most needed is not the mere reiteration
of those facts, even if more ably and con-
vincingly stated, but rather to show by careful
and discriminating statistics to what extent
girls have been injured, beyond boys, by the

system. Dr. Clarke does not marshal his facts in any such way as this, and in some cases almost commits direct unfairness by the omission, — as, for instance, where he cites " Bits of Talk," to show the superior physique of the Nova Scotia children as compared with those of New England, and forgets to state that the italics he introduces are his own, and that the author of that book does not emphasize the superiority in the one sex more than in the other.

It has been pointed out, again and again, in the " Woman's Journal " and elsewhere, that there are whole classes of facts to be had, bearing most closely on this question, which neither Dr. Clarke nor any physiologist opposed to co-education has yet attempted to obtain. Instead of shrinking from these facts, we are constantly begging for them. Until they are obtained, systematized, and displayed, the whole argument of Dr. Clarke has but an insufficient basis of facts. They are such as these : —

1. We need facts as to *the comparative physiology of American women in different localities.*

form the sturdy German fräulein and robust English damsel into the fragile American miss." (p. 168.)  How does he know it could not ?  I have seen this change very nearly effected, in a single generation, among the children of English, Irish, French Canadians, and even the Nova Scotians whom he so praises ; and this in families where even reading and writing were rare accomplishments.  As far as I can observe, the effect of climate, change of diet, change of living, on all these classes, is almost sure to produce the same result of delicacy, almost of fragility, in the second generation, with or without schooling ; and among the boys almost as much as among the girls.  A physician in a large manufacturing town once told me that the unhealthiest class of the community, in his opinion, consisted of the sons of Irish parents.

3. We need also *the comparative physiology of different social positions.*  As a rule, the daughters of the wealthy in America, who are sent to private schools, or taught by governesses, are far less severely taxed, as to their

brains, than the daughters of the middle classes, who go to the public schools. Is Dr. Clarke prepared to show that those of the former class are decidedly more healthy? If so, this is another point that would have a direct bearing on his argument. My own impression is that he would find it hard to prove this.

4. But there is still a fourth class of facts, only to be obtained by *an extensive record of individual instances.* Letting go all discriminations of locality, race, and social position, and looking only at individuals under similar conditions, is Dr. Clarke prepared to assert that, as a rule, it is the hardest students in the school who become invalids? He would say, on *a priori* grounds, that it must be so. But do facts show it? Looking over families and schools that I have known, I certainly cannot say that the young girls who have lost their health were the most studious, — quite as often the contrary. I have asked teachers of wide experience, " Have you observed that your best scholars have furnished the larger propor-

impress the physician, the facts of health may elude him. This beneficial influence has been well analyzed by a woman of great sense and judgment, herself a college graduate, Miss Mary E. Beedy, now residing in London. I have lately had the pleasure of reading an essay of hers, about to appear in " Scribner's Monthly," on " The Health of English and American Women." In this she incidentally gives reasons why the health of studious girls is often better than that of any others, — because their minds are happily occupied, — because they are thus kept from social excesses, far more prejudicial than study, — because their mental training improves their judgment and self-control, — and because they are less reckless about their health in proportion as they have an object to gain. I quote these points from memory. Coming from a graduate of Antioch College, they are surely entitled to consideration ; and yet all the thought and observation of Dr. Clarke had not suggested one of these points to his mind. If he had thought of them, he would surely have mentioned them ; for they were essential to the justice of his statement.

It seems to me fair to point out, also, the insufficient way in which Dr. Clarke presents his authorities, when he goes outside of his own observations. The single statement which I have seen cited from his book, by the newspapers, twice as often as all others put together, is his citation of the opinion of " a philanthropist and an intelligent observer," that " the co-education of the sexes is intellectually a success, physically a failure." Yet Dr. Clarke does not give the name of this informant, nor any thing but the vaguest hint as to the extent or value of his observations. The gentleman to whom the remark has been, I find, popularly attributed, Rev. C. H. Brigham, of Ann Arbor, Michigan, expressly disclaims it in a private letter to me, and he has recently published a statement looking quite the other way. Dr. Clarke also states that " another gentleman, more closely connected with a similar institution of education than the person just referred to, has arrived at a similar conclusion." (p. 144.) I must say, with due deference to Dr. Clarke, that this does not seem to me a scientific way of adducing evidence. During the hurry and excitement of the first days of our civil war, it was considered worth while to telegraph all over the country the opinions of "a reliable gentleman" or the statements of "an intelligent contraband;" but we do not find such authorities gravely cited in the official reports of the "Surgical Results of the War."

It seems to me, therefore, that Dr. Clarke by no means comes up to the recognized standard of science either in the quantity or the quality of the facts on which he bases his argument. But, granting his premises sufficient, is his conclusion just?

## II. *Dr. Clarke's Inferences.*

In a first article on Dr. E. H. Clarke's work " Sex in Education," some criticisms were made on his statements of fact ; and it was pointed out that all the cases actually cited by him, of special injury to the health of women through school education, amounted to precisely five. Since writing that article I have visited Vassar College, where I found a good deal of dissatisfaction to exist among the authorities, over one of those five cases, as stated by Dr. Clarke. He mentions a certain Miss D. who entered Vassar College at fourteen. The President and the Resident Physician assured me that no pupil had ever entered that institution at that age. Dr. Clarke says of this young lady that " she studied, recited, stood at the blackboard, walked, and went through her gymnastic exercises, from the beginning to the end of the term, just as boys do." The same authorities told me that this statement, taken as a whole, was an absolute untruth ; the gymnastic exercises being

absolutely forbidden to the students at certain
periods, and the greatest care being enjoined
upon them in all respects. The President and
the Resident Physician also expressed some
surprise that, in a case of such importance, their
testimony should not have been at least called
for, instead of relying solely on that of the
patient. I believe that it is customary among
physicians to show some consideration or cour-
tesy to each other in such matters, before putting
cases in print which seem to reflect on the professional fidelity of any one. Be this as it may,
this denial of fundamental facts leaves this instance at least open to suspicion ; and reduces
Dr. Clarke's yet undisputed cases of injury to
the health of girls, through schooling, to four.

But suppose the instances were four thousand. Grant all his premises. What is his
conclusion ? All that he demands of an educational establishment for girls is that "the
organization of studies and instruction must
be flexible enough to admit of the periodical
and temporary absence of each pupil, without

loss of rank, or necessity of making up work, from recitation and exercise of all sorts." (p. 158.) And yet he goes on to declare that for Harvard College, for instance, to adapt itself for the introduction of young women, would be a thing so enormously difficult that it would cost two millions of dollars! (p. 151.)

This is what is so inexplicable to me in the conclusions of the book. Grant all Dr. Clarke's facts, and all his demands, — what follows? Of course, in that case, those grammar schools and high schools to which girls are admitted must be essentially remodelled. These I waive. But, so far as our leading colleges are concerned, — and Harvard in particular, — I not only do not see why the remodelling for the admission of women should cost two millions, but I do not see why it should cost a cent. I do not see, indeed, why there is needed at Harvard any remodelling at all : only a quiet carrying out of what is already the marked tendency in that institution, — to substitute elective for required studies, voluntary attendance on exercises for required attendance, and examinations as tests of scholarship in place of daily marks. Surely it cannot have escaped Dr. Clarke's notice that if he were having Harvard College arranged on purpose to suit girls, according to his formula just quoted, it could hardly be done by a more effectual process than is actually going on at this moment, without any reference to women at all. If this be so, why not extend this new system to women and let them have the benefit of it?

When Dr. Clarke and I were in Harvard College, every absence from daily prayers or recitation counted as an offence. Now each student is allowed sixty absences from prayers, — almost one-fourth of the whole number, — and no questions are asked until that number is exceeded. Then almost all rank turned on marks given at the daily recitation. Now there are departments in which no daily marks are given, and the question of scholarship is determined by occasional examinations. To these, it would seem, Dr. Clarke does not object, for he says (p. 134) " it is easy to frame a theoretical emulation, in which results only are compared and tested, that would be healthy and invigorating." Yet such emulation as this is all that seems likely to be left at Harvard in the way of dangerous rivalry, when the present system shall have been fully developed. "The steady, untiring, day-by-day competition" that Dr. Clarke deprecates is being utterly laid aside ; and a more flexible system is being introduced for young men, which turns out to have also the incidental advantage of being precisely what young women need.[1]

It is a valuable discovery that, the more you transform a college into a University, the better it is adapted for both sexes. The same advantage may be noted on another point, the con-

[1] An additional illustration of this is in the resolution introduced at the meeting of Harvard Overseers, Dec. 30, 1873, and since adopted : —

"*Resolved*, That the Board of Overseers consents that for the academic year 1874–5 all rules imposing penalties or marks of censure upon Seniors for absences from church, and from recitations, lectures, or exercises other than examinations, be suspended."

3          D

sideration of which may throw light on Dr. Clarke's demand for two million dollars. I mean the question of dormitories. If the admission of girls to our colleges does nothing else but to break down the present system of brick barracks, and to substitute the simpler boarding-house system of Michigan University, it will be a work well done. Of course, if there must be duplicated for girls the vast array of dormitories now encumbering the scanty college-yard at Cambridge, it will cost a great deal of money. But just now, when all the boarding-house keepers of Cambridge are deploring their occupation gone by reason of these structures, it is the very time to introduce young women into the humbler quarters left vacant ; and why, in this case, will these students cost the college more than so many additional young men ? Once adopt the plan, which I believe to be the true one, that it is simply the office of the college to provide facilities of instruction, and that of the pupils and their parents (under the general supervision of the college) to look out for food and

lodging, medical attendance and spiritual guid-
ance, — and the increased expense of joint collegiate education turns out a mere chimera.
Were it ever so great, I should still regard it as
the best way of spending money, since, in any
case, the expense of providing for girls equal
advantages in a separate college would be still
greater ; but I do not see it to be great, or
indeed to amount to any thing worth mentioning
at all. Nor do I see why, even if we admit all
Dr. Clarke's facts, he has given a single valid
reason why our colleges should not admit girls
to-morrow, — making, as many of them have
already made on other grounds, the necessary
changes to secure sufficient flexibility of system.

It therefore seems to me that, as his facts are
not worked out with sufficient thoroughness to
justify any general conclusion whatever, so his
conclusion that our present colleges, and particularly Harvard College, cannot, except at a
vast expense, admit women, is utterly unsus-
tained by his facts.

## III.

### BY MRS. HORACE MANN.

DR. CLARKE's "Sex in Education" would have been an invaluable addition to popular works on hygiene, if it had been written in a different spirit, — without insult to woman, whom the author professes to respect, and whom he pronounces to be capable of as extended education as men are. This admission on his part is actually overlooked by many of his reviewers, because their feelings are so hurt by his ungentlemanly jeers, and his vulgar attack upon the noble army of unmarried women, who are often in the respectable ranks of "spinsterism," as he calls it, out of self-respect, and because their ideal of the marriage state is far beyond that of the average woman.

The average woman has unfortunately been educated to consider matrimony more respectable than the state of single blessedness, which has thus been well named when compared with the heartless or heart-breaking condition of incompatible or unworthy marriage. Probably not one of these women would have refused marriage if the conditions she required had been fulfilled, but without these her self-respect would have been compromised. Probably the sentiment of love has been awakened in the breasts of all. It would be unnatural, I concede, if it were not so.

> " God gives us love,
>     Something to love he lends us ; "

but it is far better for the soul to live in an ideal union with a possible twin-soul than to enter marriage upon a low plane of thought or feeling. When this most vital institution of society is demoralized by worldliness, cupidity, or other of the manifold forms of selfishness, the greatest unhappiness is sure to follow ; on the principle that the corruption of the best is the worst. It is in this fatal disappointment of life that we see the undeveloped women ; and many a young woman, who has an opportunity to make the observation, is made cautious of trusting her happiness to what appears to be, and has justly been called, "the lottery of life." It seems incredible that a man who has had Dr. Clarke's opportunity of seeing domestic life has not realized that unfortunate marriages are the circumstances under which the harmonious development of nature is arrested and perverted. Such circumstances stunt growth and spoil family life, and the children who are its unhappy result. Indeed, the idea with which many women enter into the married state, even when their affections are engaged in it, pervert and maim the development of the human being, and often end in a loss of faith in human nature. This idea is that the oneness of the union is the oneness of the man, and not a new oneness born of the union. The assumption of the authority of the average husband extends even to the opinion of the wife ; so that there is often a concession to a paramount will where the wife is the superior by nature. It is the freedom from this bondage

which constitutes the happiness of single blessedness, and is at the root of the unhappy tendency to divorce which is characteristic of our
times. Far higher is the unmarried state, as
a condition for the development of the human
being, than this low state of marriage, which
latter in its ideal form is a condition of mutual
growth. A new code of morals is needed in this
regard. It is not a mere matter of speculation,
for in true marriage the ideal is realized. The
one will is only truly one when based upon perfect freedom and mutual sacrifice, — which indeed
is not conscious sacrifice, but only a loving con-
tention for self-renunciation.

I believe it is a fact that the higher the state
of civilization and refinement, the more unmarried women there are ; and yet Dr. Clarke could
add his voice to the vulgar hue and cry against
them. Such is the prevalence of this hue and
cry that women who are not elevated above its
influence by early inculcations of noble principles, of self-respect, and of a lofty ideal, rush into
matrimony because they are ashamed to appear
to be unsought.

The maternal feeling is as intense and pure in many unmarried women as in their married sisters. Indeed, if we each take an observation in our own circle, we shall see it far more developed in many of them than in many married women, to whom children are a burden and a hinderance, and always considered and treated as if of secondary importance to their pleasures, and even to their more rational pursuits. The world cannot be divided in that way. The maternal sentiment is planted in the heart of every sympathetic and affectionate woman, — indeed, woman is abnormal without it, — and, if not developed by maternity itself, this sentiment may be so by right education, and thus saved from becoming a root of bitterness such as opinions like Dr. Clarke's are calculated to plant. How many an orphan child has found the very essence of motherly feeling and life-long devotion in a maiden aunt! The man is to be pitied who has not seen this in his acquaintance with society : one almost wishes to cite names to prove one's words. Has Dr. Clarke no touch-stone within himself to prove such characters, — for he must have seen many of them ? The maternal feeling is often more judiciously exercised where the passion of maternity — what some moralists have called brute maternity — has not been roused into activity by actual motherhood. I would farther explain this by a reference to those mothers in whom every other sentiment, even that of good wifehood, is absorbed by the maternal feeling ; and where, if they are undisciplined in mind, this feeling makes it impossible for them to see the faults of their children, or to allow any one else to note them, or give them any aid in their correction. Even the father is deprived of his natural right to share in the care, and is treated as their natural enemy if he criticises them. The loving but unimpassioned aunt, or co-operating educator, whose maternal feeling has been cultivated by her vocation, can see the facts more clearly than such mothers, and can often suggest the remedies. I think it may safely be asserted that the first proof of improvement in the popular feeling about marriage

3*

practically engaged in education. I make it
more earnestly than ever, for education is not
merely the knowledge of sciences, languages, or
systems of philosophy, but consists in the use of
the faculties and their application to life thus
developed by these and other studies. "The
proper study of mankind is man," is an utterance that has often been quoted to prove that
the exact sciences were inferior objects of pursuit to the study of language and philosophy ;
but man cannot be studied aright without a scientific basis, and this is the greatest argument
for the complete education of women, in whose
hands is the moulding of the human race. When
they do not hold their normal place and function, — which they cannot do if uncultivated, —
the condition of such portions of the human
race shows it palpably.

But I must not, like many of Dr. Clarke's
reviewers, forget that he concedes woman's right
and her capacity for the most extended education.

Let us now look at facts in regard to the danger of systematic and persistent study for women. One would think, judging by Dr. Clarke's "dreadful little book," as some one has called it, that women had generally been educated to death, while the deplorable fact is that she has only been half educated at the best. When in those instances, few and far between, where high culture was desired, the time for real study has come, the necessity for making up for former deficiencies has sometimes made it too severe. In half a century's acquaintance with the details of female education, I can remember no instance in which study has proved injurious to those who came to it in good health : excepted cases are truly exceptional, and not the average. I have also known instances where young women who were invalids have made a studious life their recreation, and have gained health and vigor meanwhile, — all the happier and better for the intellectual life.

The best remedy for too hard study at any one time of life is a thorough and gradual mental training from childhood up. The earliest education of both boys and girls is, generally speaking, aimless and indefinite. A certain amount of reading, writing, arithmetic, and geography are considered necessary, but instruction in these is not in itself cultivation of mind. It may be perfectly arbitrary and wooden, done without any reference to or attempt to develop the nature. Even reading and writing need not be taught so mechanically as is done in the schools. Very little attention is given usually in American schools to the subject-matter of the reading: each child is called upon to read a sentence or a paragraph, in a reader, instead of having a work of genius put into its hands, which is to be read in company, and which is interesting enough in itself to chain the attention and to bring out the natural elocution by making the rest listen while one reads.* Geography is usually taught by map and outline, with little or no

---

* In making this criticism, and other possible ones, upon the schools, I ought not to forget that one teacher is expected to minister to the mental wants of fifty, and sometimes even of a hundred scholars, — a relic of barbarism which it is hoped that time will ameliorate.

descriptive or picturesque explanation of scenery, fauna, or remarkable natural features ; and arithmetic in as uninteresting a way, instead of being made living by being connected with geometrical science. Children's industrial faculties are not set at work, and the whole routine becomes tedious, is disconnected with life, and is shirked as much as possible. Very little training in the native language is given, and even in the most advanced public schools little attention is paid to the art of writing down thoughts and impressions, — an exercise which can with advantage be begun in childhood. Boys and girls begin to study Latin thus without an interesting idea about human speech.

Boys are at last set to work systematically to prepare for their higher education, and every aid is given them to make up for lost time. Girls sometimes share this training for a little while in some places ; but, as it leads to nothing in particular, it soon loses its interest, unless perchance they are preparing to be teachers. Girls rarely go far in mathematical studies, which are the basis of all scientific education; and, if they study what are called the higher branches in schools, without this thorough mathematical training that boys have, it is very superficial study, and soon forgotten. In the exceptional cases, consisting of those whose strong native talent and favoring circumstances urge on to hard study, the necessity of making up for lost time may injure the weak, and even break down the strong, as is often the case with men. I do not believe the overstraining of the brain is any more injurious to young women than to young men, and it is not a thousandth part so common. The evil effects that appear at that time of life in both sexes are due to other causes than those Dr. Clarke points out so exclusively. He says there are other causes, but he passes them over lightly. One of his reviewers has pointed them out ably and in detail. As far as they refer to study, the system of cramming and emulation, in both public and private schools, should bear the brunt of his accusations. It would undoubtedly testimony to the success and good effects of co-education, as well as to the possibility of harmonious persistent study for women.

The only feature of it that was ever objectionable in my eyes has been the gathering of young girls into the preparatory school, where they could enter at the age of twelve. It is unfortunate enough to be obliged to send young boys away from home, but it is far more objectionable to send young girls away. They ought to live at home while getting their preparatory education, and all the more if they are to follow it up with college life. Domestic life is made null to them thus. The only apology for having a preparatory school of the kind there was the fact that so many people live scattered in the West that schools are not accessible to them, and the preparation required for a college course could be obtained in no other way. My heart used to ache for the lovely little girls, separated from their mothers at an age when they should have been in their arms every night, with all those little

E

confidences and confessions that mothers only can elicit. No matron could supply the mother's place, even if devoted solely to the office of mothering the children of a large boarding-school.

But the case was very different with the young women who came to take a course of college study. With an occasional exception, they were of an age and maturity of character that made them competent to take care of themselves. One of the chief principles of that college discipline was the absence of all emulation as a motive power. There were no honors to be studied for, there was not even a rank list to show comparative progress, there was no competition for pre-eminence in college graduation, for every student was called upon to prepare himself or herself to speak ; and when the graduating class was large the speakers were determined by lot, and not by choice. No pupil necessarily knew how a fellow - pupil stood. If ill-health interrupted study, time and opportunity were given to make up the deficiencies without any publicity; so that Dr. Clarke's objections to co-education on that score fall to the ground, as far as that college is concerned. The mental and moral influences of the mutual college life were very marked in the superior moral deportment and refinement of manners in the young men, and the un-excited and modest demeanor of the young women, both meeting with mutual respect for each other's intellectual and social claims. One or two instances of extravagant ambition for scholarship, and still more for dispatch, were the only cases of failure in health among the young women; and these were not sanctioned or promoted by any stimulus from the president or professors. One ambitious teacher in the department of the preparatory school, who wished the pupils in her classes to make a greater show than others, was duly checked by interference from the seats of authority. The health of both the young men and women improved in a marked manner during their college life. Many came with no knowledge of hygiene or their own physiological need, and special instruction was given in those branches of knowledge. The health of the girls was much better than that of the young men.

Young women who came with their systems out of order, through ignorance and unhealthy living, were greatly benefited, and sent home to spread the knowledge they had gained. But one death of each sex occurred in six years (the period of which I write), and they were both cases of poisoning by food in metallic vessels ; yet the hardships were great during the first years, and the exposures rather exceptional, owing to the poverty of the food and the inadequacy of the buildings as to ventilation and water supply.

Regular occupation and mental activity are as good for women as for men. Dr. Clarke probably judges of women by the invalids he has tended ; and his observations have been chiefly limited, to all appearance, to the unhealthful life and habits of cities. It cannot be hard study that has chiefly injured the young women he has known, for I suspect few have ever undertaken it. It has been late hours, fashionable dress, with its necessary sacrifice of warmth and ease, hot houses and school-rooms, and unnatural cramming to meet the demands of unhealthy emulation.

The educators of our private institutions for girls will testify that they have found it difficult to induce their pupils to a continuous and thorough course of study. The demands of society, as it is called, have been allowed to interfere ; and fashionable schools have lived by fashion rather than by merit. One of the ablest teachers of a private high school in Boston testified that her school suddenly rose to unexampled popularity without any internal changes, because one or two fashionable girls entered it ; and it as suddenly settled back to its usual numbers because they and their followers left it in dudgeon for some cause. All such educators know the frail tenure upon which they hold their city schools ; and even gentlemen who have taught young ladies' schools have experienced the same sudden reverses. In the late movement for higher education in Boston, one of the most earnest women in the cause, when it was suggested to her that the girls in high life did not, as far as educators could judge, care for higher education, replied, "We must make it fashionable, and then they will care for it."

No, the demand comes from a very different quarter, — from those whose means cannot command facilities to meet literary, artistic, or scientific aspirations, and who are willing to make sacrifices for education. If Dr. Clarke had assailed the abuses of society, — children's parties, fashionable dress in its features of bare neck and limbs, thin shoes, sudden change of costume, late hours, and a thousand hardships and exposures to which the less favored classes of society are subjected, — he would have done better service than by discouraging women's systematic education, and throwing obstacles in the path of their culture. Still deeper, I would again testify, is the wrong he has done to women by assailing those who devote noble lives to charity, to their own culture and to the culture of others, and whom those who know them feel would be profaned by worldly marriages. The children they act for rise up and call them blessed, and by their affection go far toward making up to them for the lost rapture of actual motherhood.

## IV.

### BY ADA SHEPARD BADGER.

No thoughtful reader can fail to appreciate the nobleness of the purpose that actuated Dr. Clarke in writing " Sex in Education." No loving and thinking mother can lay aside the book, after reading the first pages, until the whole is perused. But no candid woman teacher, with the interests of education for girls deeply at heart, can quietly allow Dr. Clarke's statement to pass without wishing to suggest essential modifications of its main idea.

In her double capacity of teacher and mother, the writer of the present article begs leave to call the attention of other mothers and teachers to a few facts bearing upon the other side of this *quæstio vexata.*

And, to begin with that branch of the subject which is least essential, since *education* stands before *co-education* in all minds,— and, so that we obtain the former, we will not insist too strongly upon the latter, — Dr. Clarke quotes the opinion of " a philanthropist and an intelligent observer," holding an official connection with a college for men and women, that " the co-education of the sexes is intellectually a success, physiologically a failure." He does not state the facts from which this inference is drawn. Doubtless this observer has known instances where women who studied in classes with men finally succumbed to disease, as did some of their male classmates, in all probability.

But what gives him the power to decide that the proportion of the sufferers among the female graduates is greater than that among their male classmates, or that the seeds of the particular form of malady which has prostrated any woman student were not sown, before the birth of the latter, in the organism of a mother to whose youth the opportunity for a liberal education was denied ? And how can he know that their very origin was not attributable to the lack of that

4

knowledge of physiology requisite to instruct a woman as to the commonest facts with regard to the care of herself required by the approach of the sacred office of maternity ? And what probability is there that, had the sufferer in question pursued one of the *alternatives* to a student's course, a life of fashionable folly, or even one of common toiling, uninspired by the light of a newly awakened intellectual life, these germs of disease would have been less likely to come to fruition ? What are the grounds of belief that regular study is a prominent cause of physical degeneracy ?

Facts of the nature of those stated by Dr. Clarke (in Part III., chiefly clinical) would doubtless be adduced by the observer above cited, were he called upon to substantiate his opinion. But, could we look at any one of these cases with the power to judge the hidden as well as the revealed causes in operation, considering also what would have been the probable alternative adopted by the individual in question, had study not been her chief pursuit, is it not quite possible that the conclusion at which we should arrive would contradict that of the work before us ?

One of the most striking cases mentioned in Part III. chances to have been known to the writer from the earliest infancy of the subject. And, although the details of such a case are forbidden by many considerations, the circumstance of studying in and being graduated with honor at a college planned for both sexes, and in which, indeed, she remained through the senior year only, was but a slight cause among the many that converged to menace, and finally to overcome, that rarely endowed but perilously poised organization. The congenial pursuit of the studies that were so large a part of her life probably delayed for years a result that discerning observers saw imminent for her from the dawning of her conscious life. Neither "death from over-work," nor "death from unphysiological work," was a verdict to pass unchallenged in her case.

Who that looked upon Story's bust of Elizabeth Browning could come away without a sympathetic tingling, as it were, of the whole being, from the possibilities of suffering — beyond the conception of most mortals — revealed in that exquisitely sensitive face?

But Mrs. Browning did not go to a man's college, or to any college. She studied with her father at home, and could take all the rests required by the needs of her physical life. No college routine, but, possibly, the very absence of its regularity, was responsible for her sufferings throughout her life. God wrote on her organism the lines that could not be effaced by time or circumstance.

Yet she could write, in that patient sweetness which was more wonderful than her version of "Prometheus Bound," or her "Drama of Exile," and which made her a glorious woman more essentially than a gifted poet : —

> "Oh ! we live, — Oh ! we live, —
> And this life that we conceive
> Is a strong thing and a grave,
> Which for others' use we have,
> Duty-laden to remain.

We are helpers, fellow-creatures,
Of the right against the wrong : —
We are earnest-hearted teachers
Of the truth that maketh strong, —
Yet do we teach in vain ? ''

No generalizations can be drawn from one
case, or from seven cases, of women who have
become invalids after working continuously "in
a man's way." Far more numerous cases might
be cited, by physicians and teachers, of girls who
were seized upon by the Proteus of disease, as
a retribution, let us think, for not having worked
with the *method* of "a man's way," or for not
having worked at all. Nowhere in our own
country does the average woman present so
feeble and diseased an aspect as in those parts
of the West and South where education is of the
smallest moment to her. Lacking the delicate
beauty and the intellectual tastes of the New
England girl, she also leads a life of greater
physical suffering, and a more hopeless inca-
pacity for usefulness. Is unremitting study a
cause of the weakness of the Georgia planter's
wife or the Cincinnati merchant's daughter ?

Facts in the writer's possession, through an intimate acquaintance, during the first ten years of its existence, with one of our Western colleges, established for the joint education of the sexes, are somewhat significant as indicating whether, notwithstanding the many difficulties under which this infant college was obliged to struggle on, the education there given to girls was destructive or constructive. Out of twenty-seven women graduates (all that memory can recall in the absence of catalogues which might permit a full statement), nineteen have married, and eight have remained unmarried, so far as the writer knows. Out of these twenty-seven, graduating between 1857 and 1863, one only has died. All but three, whose post-graduate history has been unreported, are known to have done effective work, for a longer or shorter term of years, in educational and other departments ; and a large number of them have blooming families to "rise up and call them blessed." The writer has never heard of but three cases of even temporary invalidism among these women graduates, while a large number of the male students of the same classes have died, or been prostrated by grievous maladies. One of the three cases just referred to was the indisposition for some months of a lady who has since recovered ; and who has recently taken her eldest son to Germany, to pursue there her favorite study of music, to which she has consecrated, as pupil and teacher, a great part of her time for over twenty years. Another, confessedly bearing away the first honors of a class in which were graduated two of our successful Unitarian preachers, is now rearing a rosy family of boys on the shore of a Western lake, having taught most successfully for years in a high school.

Another, yet unmarried, is continuing her studies in England, where her rare powers and ripe culture are winning for her the appreciation she years ago won from that long-time friend of a wise co-education, the editor of the " Liberal Christian," who wrote of her in glowing terms from St. Louis, the former field of her work.

Another of these graduates, the mother of six

remarkably fine, healthy children, is giving her
husband the most efficient assistance in his work
at the head of a Theological School in Eastern
New York.

Here, then, is a class of facts, small, it is true,
but significant as to some not unhappy results
of a liberal education for women, even though
obtained "in a man's way." "By their fruits
ye shall know them," said another Good Physician.

"In the development of the organization is to
be found the way of strength and power for both
sexes," says Dr. Clarke. "Limitation or abor-
tion of development leads to weakness and
failure."

Had these women been denied the privileges
of education which their natures craved so earnestly that they were willing, in some cases, to go
alone to a distant State ; to borrow money to
defray their school expenses, so that the first-
fruits of their after-work went to cancel these
arrearages ; to give up the attractions of life in
New England, at the age when its charms are

most alluring ; to spend, in a new country, in privation and close study, years that might otherwise have been squandered in dissipation or wasted in futile attempts to teach at the enormous disadvantage of inadequate preparation ; had these women been denied the education they struggled for and obtained in the only way then possible, who knows what hydra-headed maladies might now be racking their bodies and distracting their brains ? Study, severe study, if you will, was their safeguard, not their peril, even in a physical point of view.

Dr. Clarke justly — shall we say generously ? — concedes the right of women to the highest culture of which they are capable. But the point of his argument turns upon the *method* of obtaining this culture. And just here, in a man's view of the case, seems a mighty difficulty arising. But put one or two wise, mother-ly women on the faculty of each college where girls are admitted, (and what advocate for the liberal culture of women would think of sending girls to study where men alone preside ?) and

woman's wit will speedily solve the great problem of " the periodical remission from labor."

Assume that each girl student must rest
entirely from brain-work three days out of every
thirty, and the average of work could be easily
brought up by a little exercise of common sense
on the part of teacher and pupil. But it is not
to be assumed that every girl, or that one girl
out of ten, must rest three days, or even one
day, out of thirty. Not unfrequently girls who
afterwards developed into sound, healthy matrons,
standing the wear and tear of life in a manner to
astonish vigorous men hardly able to hold their
own in the rush of our American life, have been
known to attend, without a single exception,
every recitation of their classes for years, even
when going daily from quite a distance to school
or college. A moderate and regular use of the
mental faculties, such as should alone be permitted in our schools and colleges, with ample
margins each week for the exigencies of life for
both sexes, has been again and again proved to
be conducive to the highest physical health for
women as well as men.

A few years ago a young girl of sixteen, who had left school under a physician's advice, because of certain irregularities in her physical health, was rapidly passing into such a state of apathy to things ordinarily attractive to the young, that wise friends feared the result of insanity. As a last resort, she was placed in a school where, amid pleasant companionship, her faculties were gently though regularly stimulated. She soon began to revive under a regimen of mathematics, languages, and art-culture, and in two years was in a state of perfect health. During these entire two years she was not absent from school more than three times, nor did she ever fail to prepare a lesson. Here regularity of study was not a source of disease, but, apparently, its cure.

But the instances in point, thronging the mind of the writer, would tax the patience of the reader unjustifiably. Passing over those omissions and oversights in the book, so happily specified in notices like that of the " Advertiser " and the " Liberal Christian," a few words more must close this already too long reference to this timely and, in many respects, valuable essay.

The evil to which our wise and kind physician refers, is surely not to be overlooked. It exists; it stares at us from early graves, and, far worse, from homes whose central figures are afflicted with life-long sufferings before which the stoutest-hearted men might quail.

What is its remedy? Does our earnest-hearted friend propose one which the exigencies of life will permit women to adopt? Has any writer suggested a cure for this menacing ill?

If a warning trumpet is to be blown, shall no one be found to herald also the hope of better things?

Let a woman's voice be heard pleading, not for less work or less constant work, but for a wiser method of work in our schools! Let a ban be put upon public exhibitions of both boys and girls in schools! Let the worry arising from a false system of marks for recitations, and from all comparisons and competitions, be banished forever! Let the notion that girls must recite all their lessons while standing vanish from the minds of both teachers and physicians! The use of the feet is not essential to a good translation from Homer or Goethe; and even the Calculus has been mastered by students who, for the most part, sat at recitations. Let evening parties, and the various forms of tempting amusements which beset our young people while attending to the serious work of their education, be as strictly forbidden to them as they are to their infant brothers and sisters yet in the nursery! Let the tyrannous fashion-plate be consulted less than the laws of harmonious coloring and real fitness of contour!

Above all, let the beginnings be right! Remember that far more valuable work can be done for the education of any human being, and especially of a girl, by reason of her threefold nature, between the ages of seven and fourteen than between fourteen and nineteen. Let our girls remain girls till they have reached the estate of womanhood. Let their development be gradual and normal, not forced and spasmodic; and we shall have no hothouse flowers to fade and die at the first touch of the ruder air of real life, but blossoms that are the pledge of coming fruit.

It would be unjust and ungrateful in any woman not to recognize the fact that Dr. Clarke's book was necessarily written in haste, in hours snatched from his absorbing labors in alleviating the sufferings of those for whose good he wrote. It was doubtless this haste that rendered possible such a verbal error as occurs on page 35, where he hides the venerable Ulysses, instead of the youthful Achilles, among the maidens.

In conclusion, we would insist not only that the diseases so often referred to do not originate generally in the schools, but that the only way in which they can be reached and cured is through the instruction imparted and the regularity of life, in all its details, required by wisely conducted schools, covering the whole period from early girlhood to full maturity.

## V.

### BY CAROLINE H. DALL.

"THE hand of iron in the glove of silk!" How utter one word in the face of testimony like this, — honest, conscientious, earnest; adding to the highest professional reputation all the force of a pure and noble individual character? How do it, still further, in the face of personal obligations accumulating for more than twenty years, and of that loving respect with which the physician who is also priest is held in every household? I have anticipated this book with pain. I lay it down with pain, far sharper and far different from any that I foresaw. I start from the same premises with Dr. Clarke; for I believe the spiritual and intellectual functions of men and women to tend differently to their one end; and their development to this end, through the physical, to be best achieved by different methods   But I do not believe that any greater difference of capacity, whether physical or psychical, *will be* found between man and woman than *is* found between man and man ; and my faith in the co-education of the sexes has been greatly stimulated by the present inelastic method, from which many boys *do* shrink as much as any girl *could.*

Under a proper system boys and girls help each other forward, not merely towards excellent scholarship, but towards a perfect humanity, — that is, a perfect self-possession, — the attainment for each of a sound mind in a sound body.   To understand this, however, not even the President of Harvard will find possible unless he does more than *look* at a mixed college. To have any fair comprehension of the elements which constitute its power for good or evil, it is necessary to pass at least a week within its walls, sharing the " college commons " and the college recreations ; studying its whole action as if it were a large family.

When I laid down this book I felt the emphasis of my pain in a direction wholly unexpected. Every woman who takes up her pen to reject its conclusions knows very well that it will penetrate hundreds of households where her protest cannot follow ; and Dr. Clarke must be patient with the number and weight of our remonstrances, since he knows very well that upon the major part of the community our words will fall with no authority, our experiences invite no confidence. We must gain the public ear by constant iteration, and by our " importunity " prevail. This book will fall into the hands of the young, and that I deplore. They should be taught the proper care of their growing bodies ; but any such cases of disease as are here recorded are fruitful of evil stimulus to any girl inclined to hysterics. If this subject ought to be discussed publicly at all, a matter open to doubt, teachers and mothers should discuss it. No amount of professional skill can avail in place of that sympathetic intuition of causes which should spring from identical physical constitution. In no pages that I ever read is the need of educated women physicians so painfully apparent as in these. I expected to find premises from which I should dissent, but, with the exception of that upon which the book is based, I did not find any; and, so far as it is an argument against co-education, the book utterly fails.

Co-education does not necessarily include identical methods; and, if it did, Dr. Clarke's examples of broken constitutions are brought from the clerk's desk, the theatre, and the woman's college, as well. His examples have no statistical value; for nothing is told us of their proportion to the whole number of students of the other sex under the same precise conditions, or to the failures in the same number of girls educated tenderly at home. When the book passes from the methods of education to the effect of those methods on womanly functions, the treatment of the subject is both one-sided and incomplete. The only proper place for a discussion of the latter *in extenso* is the columns of a medical journal; but this book is intended for popular use, and to the people must those who criticise it appeal.

The most painful thing in the book is its *tone.* Mr. Higginson has said that it is not *coarse !* Surely never was a sentence written that more eloquently betrayed the need women have to speak for themselves ! Women read this essay with personal humiliation and dismay. A certain materialistic taint is felt throughout the whole, such as saddens most of our intercourse with our young physicians, but which we had hoped never to associate with this man, so long and so justly revered. The natural outgrowth of this tone are the sneers which disfigure its pages, the motto from Plautus, and a few most unhappy illustrations.

These things might be easily forgiven to the immature student, as we pardon the rude manners of growing boys ; but should not our friend have denied himself the small relief of their utterance ? We cannot excuse the trait merely because the work has been undertaken in the midst of more pressing cares. We feel that it indicates something in the author which is no accident. We do not accept it as suitable in the " beloved physician " for whose delicate and thoughtful care so many have been grateful. He, at least, should have given us pages that a woman might read without a blush.

We are sorry that he thought it worth while to invent a word to give point to his sneer. If there are any " agenes " in the world, surely we do not find them in the women who, seeking to do some good work in the world, have sought the development of their best powers in ways unwise or absurd, and have in consequence failed to satisfy the yearnings that they feel. " Other tasks in other worlds " await them, and the yearning may still prove the germ of a completed development. The true " agenes " are the men who have lost manhood through vicious courses, and whose innocent wives will never hear the voices of their children in consequence. We look from the possible mother to the father, and I mean all that my words imply. It is the testimony of one even more familiar with the nursery and the sick-room than with the theories of the platform. The vices of *men* imperil the populations of the earth far more than the unwise studies of women.

Very painful, also, is the witness these pages bear to the small number of wise and noble mothers among us, — women who can so impress themselves upon their daughters that they should follow modest and wholesome courses, as if by instinct or habit, and should shrink from all the possible unwomanly exposure which has made these pages necessary. Our author quotes a letter from a German mother, as if it could not have been written here. But the mothers of all my schoolmates lived as if they had written it, and it gives the experience of that portion of present society who believe in motherly influence and exercise motherly care. It is true that there are "fast" young women, with whom the restraints of proper feeling do not prevail; but distinctions should be made in the writing. Refined and thoughtful women should be credited with their actual habits.  Dr. Clarke has lost a most precious opportunity.  It was in his power to stamp the objectionable mode of life with its real vulgarity.  If *any* fathers would but guard their sons as many women still know how to guard their daughters!  The revelations of this book are enough to chill any one with horror.

In the writing of this book acknowledged statistics seem to have been wholly overlooked.  More female infants than male survive the perils of infancy, and more girls mature into womanhood than boys into manhood.  Will any one who looks carefully at the immature half-developed figures of our young men, or keeps the record of *their* vitality, claim that it is superior to that of women?

In all books that concern the education of women, one very important fact is continually overlooked.

Women, and even young girls at school, take their studies *in addition* to their home-cares.  If boys are preparing for college, they do not have to take care of the baby, make the beds,

were a new thing, whereas the second generation born upon these shores bore witness to it.
It was observed by travellers one hundred and
fifty years ago. As to the endurance of the
duties of motherhood, and the proportion of
surviving children born to them, our women are
far in advance of the first generation, born and
reared across the water. It was a rare thing in
that generation for man and wife to live together
through the whole natural period of conjugal life.
The men lived long ; but they had two, three,
four, and — more frequently than any one would
believe who had not examined — *five* wives. Nor
can this be accounted for on the ground that the
women were subject to uncommon hardship. The
settlers of Ipswich, for example, were wealthy ;
they built houses more comfortable than those
they had left ; and they testify that one of their
motives in coming to this country was the lack
of pure water and good drainage in the old.
Still their wives perished by the score. " The
wind at Madrid will not blow out a candle,"
says the old Spanish proverb, " but it can kill

a man." The change of climate was at the bottom of this early fatality. The condition of things steadily improved to the happy time that we all remember. If the last thirty years has checked the steady gain, let us consider patiently the era of French fashions, vices, and habits, the era of unnatural hours and pastimes. The movement in behalf of the higher education of woman is a very modern movement. No single generation can be said to have matured under its influence. It is too early to examine the results, but this is certain: whatever danger menaces the health of America, it cannot thus far have sprung from the over-education of her women.

Mrs. Badger has already shown that the health of Southern and Western women, whose opportunities of education have been small, is even lower than that of our cultivated classes, a matter easily to be tested by any one who will watch the crowd pouring out of a western railroad station. " The cerebral processes by which knowledge is acquired are the same for both sexes," says Dr. Clarke ; but observing women will hardly admit this statement. I believe it would be hardly possible for women to become students if the processes *were* identical. The slowest woman who has any real power will conquer a new study in about half the time of the average male student. Her method she does not herself understand. She has ways and means which are not apparent. I cannot believe that any " Oriental care of the body " ever equalled the care given to the women of to-day in America. The women who are now practising as physicians in the harems of Europe and Asia find fearful ignorance and absolute superstition. For myself I can only say that I look for young women of the strongest physique at this moment within the walls of academies and colleges. The regular studies, the early rising and retiring, the exercises in the gymnasium and the open air, the companionship with charming and cultivated women older than themselves, all tend to the most perfect health. This is a reproach to our homes, and perhaps indicates that carelessness in mothers which was always avoided when I was young, not so much because its results were injurious as because it was in itself unwomanly and indelicate.

Dr. Clarke fears that co-education will stimulate women to attempt what the method of their physical life renders dangerous. Why, then, does he turn from Oberlin, Antioch, and Cornell to the one institution where co-education has never been, and will never be, attempted, and where the one fact of the resident physician and the resident "lady principal" should indicate to the most careless inspection a careful adaptation to womanly needs? Or why, if he had an hysterical patient who happened to have been a pupil at Vassar, did he trust, without examination, to her statements? I may challenge an audience when I speak of Vassar; for it is against my will if it fulfil any dream of mine. From the hour that it first went into operation I have been its frequent visitor. The president and faculty might have banished me as a spy, so thoroughly committed am I to the cause of co-education. Instead they welcomed me warmly, and gave me liberty and opportunity to detect every flaw.

In a meeting of the " American Association for the Promotion of Social Science," held last May, I drew attention to the superior health of the girls at Vassar. I pointed out the fact that the health of the girls continued to improve up to the hour of graduation ; and while I had in my audience three members of the faculty, Miss Maria Mitchell, the resident physician, Dr. Avery, and President Raymond himself, it was observable that they heard me with indifference rather than pride, so perfectly familiar were they with the fact. The parents of all the pupils are also familiar with it ; and if Dr. Avery were at any moment to resign her responsible post she would receive a warm welcome in any community that had sent pupils to Vassar. The world may be challenged to produce, in any one neighborhood, four hundred young women of so great physical promise. In the following June I met Miss Mary Carpenter at Vassar by appointment. She saw with amazement how close the actual attainment of the pupils came to the curriculum proposed ; but she concluded her investigation by ejaculating, with the peculiar emphasis that all who know her will recall, "And we must admit that they have superior health, — it is most extraordinary ! " This was the testimony of one accustomed to the " rosebuds " in England's "garden of girls." In regard to the case reported by Dr. Clarke in connection with Vassar College, I was so sure that there was some mistake that I wrote at once to the resident physician, and she will be glad to be held responsible for the following statements.

The points will be perceived if the reader will refer to the 79th page of " Sex in Education." Vassar College does not receive students under fifteen, even for the first preparatory year ; and there is a preparatory course of two years. No student ever entered the freshman class at fourteen. At the beginning of every collegiate year the students are carefully instructed regarding the periodic precautions necessary to their health. They are positively forbidden to take gymnastics at all during the first two days of their period ; and, if there is the slightest diseased tendency, are told to forego those exercises entirely. They are forbidden to ride on horseback, and are strongly advised not to dance, nor to run up and down stairs, nor to do any thing else which will give successive, even though gentle, shocks to the trunk. They are encouraged to go out of doors for quiet walks and drives, and to do whatever they can to steady irritable nerves or unnatural excitement. That a student should faint again and again in the gymnasium, and still be allowed to continue her exercises there, is a statement that would not be made by any one familiar with the personal physical care given at Vassar College, not merely by the resident physician, but by the teachers acting as a body. It is a statement that will be believed by no one in the least familiar with the college methods. The faculty do not attempt to cut down the work of each

girl periodically ; but they do mean to so regulate the work of the whole time that the end of
no day shall find her overtaxed, even though
that day bear an unusual burden. The average
age of the graduates is twenty-one and one-
half. The present freshman class numbers
seventy-nine.

The girls begin the work of the year at the
following ages : —

|     |         |    |    |     |
| --- | ------- | -- | -- | --- |
| 11  | between | 20 | and | 23. |
| 14  | „       | 19 | „  | 20. |
| 23  | „       | 18 | „  | 19. |
| 24  | „       | 17 | „  | 18. |
| 6   | „       | 16 | „  | 17. |
| 1   | „       | 15 | „  | 16. |

This is a fair average class, except that it is
singular in the last item. That is almost the
only instance in the history of the college of a
student entering as a freshman under sixteen.
Few are under seventeen ; seventy-two of the
seventy-nine are over that age. Forty-eight, or
three-fifths, are over eighteen. " Eighteen,"
writes Dr. Avery, " is young enough for any
woman to begin this course. At that age, with

an average endowment of mind and body, she pursues it with gladness and ends it with rejoicing, as many of our classes can prove."

I consider this a most valuable exhibit, and it is the book before us that has called it out. Vassar never yet insisted on a " regimen not to be distinguished " from that impressed upon boys, and her pupils are guided physiologically with a watchful tenderness impossible in most homes. Such care is quite as much needed by boys. Whenever co-education becomes a fact, the social head of the mixed college must be a woman who will exercise loving motherly care for both, and who will find no practical difficulty in the natural differences.

Of one other case cited by Dr. Clarke as an instance of over or unwise education, I had an intimate and sorrowful knowledge. The degeneracy imputed to excessive culture was, in fact, the result of a tendency inherited from a vicious father, — a tendency recognized by its unfortunate subject with morbid pain from the beginning.

Nothing will pain women more in this book than the assertion that "old age is sexless." Men and women do not lose the distinctions of perfect womanhood and manhood as they draw nearer to each other, unless we are prepared to account these purely physical. A woman ceases to be a mother only to fulfil the quite as sacred functions of the grandmother. She is set free from certain cares that a large experience of life may show her all the more fit for certain other cares, both social and philanthropic ; but if she be not to her heart's core womanly, even at the age of eighty, her life has been a failure. Man, ripening alike through success and reverse, grows nearer to woman as he grows old ; but his advanced life is also worthless if it cannot offer manhood's ripest fruit to her hand. Sweet memories of happy firesides, where the winter blaze crowned snowy heads with halos, bring the quick tears to my eyes as I write. God be thanked for manhood and womanhood completed at fourscore, as I recall them ! It would seem as if Dr. Clarke can hardly yet understand what

5*

to the release. It is time that a generation of healthy *men* were provided : the occult causes lie within their own control.

The book before us may do something by rousing mothers and daughters to contemplate the situation ; but, if properly trained in wise homes towards average health, the ends of life will be far better served by the women who forget their own inconveniences and think chiefly of those endured by others.

Nothing is so absurd as to press upon a young woman's thought the idea that she is to become a mother. What if she is ? Let her make herself a healthy, happy human being, and what will may befall. What would be thought of a community which definitely undertook to train young men to the functions and duties of fathers ? A shout of derision would be raised at once. " Let us have citizens !" the world would cry. I echo the demand. Mothers are no more important to the race than fathers. We must gain both by seeking first the " kingdom of God." People should live out their young and happy days, unconscious of this issue, as the flowers take no thought of seed. This is best done when their minds are occupied with other subjects than "periodicity" or "development."

# VI.

## BY C.

A few years ago an eminent divine felt it his mission to expound to woman "the great facts of her being." He began his harangue with flattering admissions of her "intuitions" and "delicacy of taste;" and, having thus secured himself a hearing, he proceeded to declare that "woman cannot compete with man in a long course of mental labor," and that "as for training young ladies through a long intellectual course, as we do young men, it can never be done, — they will die in the process."

With the same conventional concessions to the equality of the sexes, Dr. Clarke introduces his plea for what, with great adroitness, he calls, "A Fair Chance for the Girls."

"Abstract right and wrong," he says, "has nothing to do with sex. What is right or wrong for man is equally right or wrong for woman. . . . Both have a right to do the best they can, or, to speak more justly, both should feel the duty and have the opportunity to do their best. . . . Neither is there any such thing as superiority or inferiority in the matter. Man is not superior to woman, nor woman to man. The relation of the sexes is one of equality, not of better and worse, or of a higher and lower."

"Timeo Danaos et dona ferentes."

The old doctrine of woman's sphere shines with equal clearness from the pages of Dr. Todd and Dr. Clarke, though the latter carefully avoids the obnoxious phrase. Just as plainly, though in less offensive words, does Dr. Clarke announce his belief that woman was made for man, and that maternity is her only divinely appointed mission, with an unmanly sneer at those who fail to fulfil that destiny.

The sneer is too studied to be accidental, and is to me the unpardonable sin of the book. Did the author willingly expose himself to justified attack on this point, for the express purpose of reaching the ear and heart of those superlatively weak women whom nothing can touch but a masculine sneer? Not quite believing in his own arguments, did he trust to satire to win him approval with that class of people for whom his book was written? Surely he is not so ignorant as not to know that the jeer will only weaken the argument with all thoughtful people. But was the book written for the thinking people, or for those whom ridicule, not reason, convinces? For those especially who fear masculine ridicule in all that relates to their external attractions; for those who can endure all loss save the loss of admiration; for those on whom an argument is wasted, while a sneer converts? One may fully believe that the perfection of womanhood, as of manhood, is reached in a true marriage; one may dissent from the opinion that man and woman, being equal, are therefore identical; one may not yet be fully persuaded in her own mind that the co-education of the sexes is desirable: yet if she is an earnest and thoughtful woman, as anxious for the intellectual as for the physical perfection of her sex, she must feel the gripe of the iron hand under the velvet glove in all Dr. Clarke's admissions, coupled as they are with such limitations. "Without denying the self-evident proposition," says Dr. Clarke, " that whatever a woman can do she has a right to do, the question at once arises, what can she do? and this includes the question, what can she best do? . . . The *quæstio vexata* of woman's sphere will be decided by her organization. This limits her power and reveals her divinely appointed tasks. . . . Each can do in certain directions what the other cannot; and in other directions, when both can do the same things, one sex as a rule can do them better than the other. . . . Many of the efforts for bettering her education seem to treat her as if her organization, and consequently her function, were masculine, not feminine. . . . The lily is not inferior to the rose, nor the oak superior to the clover; yet the glory of the lily is one, and the glory of the oak is another, and the use of the oak is not the use of the clover."

"Whatever a woman can do she has a right to do," is so plausible as to satisfy the credulous, were it not for the ungenerous doubt contained in the inquiry, "But what can she do? and what can she best do?"—questions which she is not to be allowed to settle for herself, but which Dr. Clarke hastens to answer by telling her "her organization limits her power, and reveals her divinely appointed tasks." She is entitled only to what she can attain as a woman; and, *being* a woman, her attainment is limited by her organization. What mother or teacher would have the heart to say to the healthy girl of fifteen, just becoming conscious of her mental powers, "My girl, hitherto you have talked, romped, chased butterflies and climbed fences, loved, hated (and studied) with your brother, with an innocent *abandon* that is ignorant of sex. Here your paths must diverge. He will go out into the world free to attain the highest mental culture of which a human being is capable. You were predestined to be a wife and a mother, and are therefore endowed with a peculiar organiza-

H

This physiological scare is the most insidious form under which the opposition to the higher education of woman has yet appeared. I speak advisedly ; for, though this book professes to be a protest against the co-education of the sexes, and even against their separate identical education, I think it will be felt by the careful reader to be a protest against any high intellectual education for women.

While the author claims to use the term education only in its broadest sense as "the drawing out and development of every part of the system," including necessarily the whole manner of life physical and psychical during the educational period, it will be seen that he lays stress only upon the physical education of girls, and upon their physical education only as it is connected with the duties of maternity. Nowhere does he hold out to the girls the promise that, if they will carefully obey his injunctions during the critical period of their lives, they can with safety, and may with propriety, seek a higher mental culture. Nowhere does he urge them finally to demand the highest mental culture, as he insists that they shall have the highest physical culture, as their birthright.

Moreover, that regimen which precludes the regular attendance of girls upon school, between the ages of fourteen and nineteen, virtually robs them of any extended course of study, since before the end of that period their so-called duties to society are thrust upon them.

Is it fair, in contrasting the ruddy cheeks and vigor of the English girl with the pallor and weakness of the American girl, to attribute the latter largely to the educational methods of our schools, and to credit nothing of the former to the simple domestic life of the English girl?

Let us "emphasize and reiterate until it is heeded" Dr. Clarke's statement that "woman's neglect of her own organization adds to the number of her many weaknesses, and intensifies their power." Let us reflect awhile before we accept his statement that "the educational methods of our schools are, to a large extent, the causes of the thousand ills that beset American women."

"Girls of bloodless skins and intellectual faces," he says, "may be seen any day, by those who desire the spectacle, among the scholars of our high and normal schools ; faces that crown, and skins that cover, curving spines which should be straight, and neuralgic nerves that should know no pain. . . . A training that yields this result is neither fair to the girls nor to the race."

Are bloodless female faces to be found only among the scholars of our high and normal schools ?

When found there, what effort has Dr. Clarke made to ascertain how much of their bloodless-ness is due to brain labor ? Does he know any thing of the home life of these girls ? Is it not just possible that they may have been defrauded of their childhood, — that in what is technically and prettily called helping their mothers, lifting and carrying baby, &c., their poor curved spines may have got a twist long before they had won admission to the high school ?

Are there no bloodless faces among the sewing girls who do not stand at their work, whose work is neither brain-work nor severe manual labor, but that most often quoted to us as the most suitable feminine occupation ?

"The number of these graduates who have been permanently disabled, to a greater or less degree, by these causes, is so great as to excite the greatest alarm," says Dr. Clarke. Will he give us the exact number, so that we need not underrate or overrate the danger ? and, if it can be proved that two out of *every* five of these wrecks to which he sadly points, were stranded on another shore than that of a sustained course of mental work, it will tend to quiet the alarm.

I do not wish to put out of sight the doctor's explicit declaration that "our school methods are not the sole causes of female weakness." He admits that "an immense loss of female power may be fairly charged" to certain delinquencies of dress and diet ; yet he as distinctly adds that, "after the amplest allowance for these, there remains a large margin of disease unaccounted for ; " that "the grievous maladies that torture a woman's earthly existence are indirectly affected by food, clothes, and exercise ; they are directly and largely affected by the methods of education in our schools." Furthermore, he makes no demand that girls shall be as carefully protected from physical strain and from mental excitement in their social life at critical periods as he does that they shall be protected from the excitements of study. A paper that, after claiming to treat upon education as "including the whole manner of life," declares the discussion of dress and similar causes of female weakness is not within its scope ; that mentions these casually as indirect causes, and is silent concerning the social excitements of girls, which every teacher feels to be a fruitful source of disease, directing its arguments mainly against their mental training, —does not seem to me to be written wholly in the interest of the girls. The writer leaves the impression, and he means to leave the impression, that the regimen of the schools, if not the sole cause, is the prime and direct cause of the cause than increased brain-work, for this degeneracy in the health of girls, they easily find it in the increased luxury and irregularity of their home life.

Teachers of long experience testify that the health of studious girls is better than that of the lazy ones, because their minds are occupied happily, and being also regularly occupied acquire a habit of concentration that is stability and strength for mind and body. The involuntary testimony of many a school-girl goes far to confirm this.

Sadder even than the bloodless skin and intellectual face of the normal-school girl is the not uncommon spectacle of the bloodless skin and unintellectual face of the girl in our fashionable private schools, whose mind has become so enervated by parental indulgence, so demoralized by constant social excitement, that, to use her own words, "the sight of a book makes her head ache."

If we could make it impossible for little girls of eight to solemnize paper-doll weddings, from

6

which the precocious guests, after refreshing themselves with lobster salad and candies, roll home in their carriages at ten at night ; if we could prevent the participation of their older sisters in private theatricals and the German, during the regular school-work of the year ; if the education of girls could be at least so far identical with that of boys that we could oppose common sense and physiological reasons to that absurd dictum of society which now thrusts girls of eighteen out of the school-room and into the matrimonial market, while their brothers of the same age are considered as mere lads and just beginning their education ; if we could take care that they are not overburdened with domestic responsibility as their brothers never are, and, instead of restricting their regular routine of school-work to the period between eight and eighteen, could extend it to the age of twenty-four, like that of their college brothers who study a profession, — the girls would have the fair chance which they now lack, both for physical and mental development.

Meantime let the well girls, and there are hundreds of them, though of course not within the Doctor's range of vision, aim for the highest intellectual culture, not deterred by the fear of being stigmatized as *agenes*.

Can any woman read this book without feeling depressed, — crushed by this cosmic law of periodicity which is to exempt her from nothing, but only to debar her from a higher education ? For the Doctor declares that "female operatives of all sorts are likely to suffer less, and actually do suffer less, from persistent work than female students, . . . because the former work their brains less." The regimen prescribed by the Doctor has so few attractions, the reward he offers is so paltry. We are to remember that "the glory of the lily is one, and the glory of the oak another." If we "pass middle life without the symmetry and development that maternity gives," we are taunted with the "hermaphroditic condition that sometimes accompanies spinsterism." We are not allowed to believe, with Alger, that "the qualities of our soul and the fruitions of our life may be perfected in spite of the relative mutilation in our lot." We are to "give girls a fair chance for physical development at school, and they will be able in after life, with reasonable care of themselves, to answer the demands made upon them." That is the summary.

Whether intentionally or not, this book panders to that sentiment of fashionable society that declares it unnecessary for girls to know any thing but to make themselves attractive; and, what is still more to be regretted, it will tend to increase the selfishness and the imaginary invalidism so prevalent among girls and women who have nothing better in life to do than to think of themselves.

The "wisely anxious" mothers do not need it; and the injudicious mothers, who wish to make the schools responsible for their own constant violation of the simplest hygienic laws in the management of their daughters, confirmed in their weakness by Dr. Clarke's leniency towards their social sins, will eagerly seize upon it as a weapon of attack.

It is easy enough to make vague and arbitrary assertions, and to point them with cruel gibes, — far easier than to prove them false. It is easy enough to meet sneer with sneer, and to animadvert upon such assertions with a certain piquancy. But neither the assertion nor the animadversion amounts to any thing without facts to support it.

A physician of such standing and authority in the community that we are compelled to listen to him has made assertions which he has not yet supported by statistics. It behooves the earnest women, especially the faithful teachers, to satisfy themselves at least whether these assertions can be supported, — in order, if they can be, to correct what is wrong in their present methods, and, if they cannot be, to do their part towards removing a false impression.

# VII.

## BY ELIZABETH STUART PHELPS.

THE only really serious thing about Dr. Clarke's book is the confusion of the author's ideas as to the precise defining line between a work adapted to popular instruction and a medical treatise. An author who forgets in the drawing-room and at the fireside that he is not in the lecture-room of the medical school, has put himself beyond the reach of knowing the real effect produced by him upon either the drawing-room or the fireside. He may have done so with the deliberate intention of a theorist who does not desire to be answered; he may have done so with the clear conscience of a zealot who desires only to do what presents itself to him as his duty. He has undoubtedly done so, at least, with motives which it were indelicate to call indelicate, whatever else might be said of them; but, all the same, he has

judgment upon a matter involving the welfare
of women can possibly be final.    His testimony,
worth what it may be worth, should seek and fall
into its proper place in the physical aspects of
such a question ; but it shall *stay* in its place.
It is but a link in a chain.    It is only a tint in a
kaleidoscope.    A question so intricate and shift-
ing as that which involves the exact position of
woman in the economy of a cursed world is not to
be settled by the most intimate acquaintance with
the proximate principles of the human frame, with
the proportions of the gray and white matter in the
brain, or with the transitional character of the
tissues and the exquisite machinery of the viscera.
The psychologist has yet his word to say.    The
theologian has a reason to be heard.    The politi-
cal economist might also add to experience knowledge.    The woman who is physically and intellectually a living denial of every premise and of
every conclusion which Dr. Clarke has advanced,
has yet a right to an audience.    Nor is he even
the man whose judgment as to the *health* of
women can be symmetrical.    No *clinical* opinion,

it will be remembered, bearing against the physical vigor of any class of people, is or can be a complete one. The physician knows sick women almost only. Well women keep away from him, and thank Heaven. If there be any well women he is always in doubt. Thousands of women will read that they are prevented by Nature's eternal and irresistible laws from all sustained activity of brain or body, but principally of brain, with much the same emotion with which we might read a fiat gone forth from the Royal College of Surgeons in London, that Americans could not eat roast beef, since their researches into morbid American anatomy had developed the fact that Americans had died of eating roast beef, as well as a peculiar structure of the American stomach, to which roast beef was poisonously adapted. Thousands of women will not believe what the author of " Sex in Education" tells them, *simply because they know better.* Their own unlearned experience stands to them in refutation of his learned statements. They will give him theory for theory. They can pile up

6*                    I

for him illustration on illustration. Statistics they have none ; but no statistics has he. They and the Doctor are met on fair fight.

Many a woman who stands at the factory loom eleven hours and a half a day, from year's end to year's end, from the age of eight to the age of forty-eight, knows better than he tells her. Every lady lecturer in the land, who unites the most exhausting kind of brain and body labor in her own experience, day and night after day and night, for the half of every year, and unites it in defiance of Dr. Clarke's prognostications, knows better. Every healthy woman physician knows better ; and it is only the woman physician, after all, whose judgment can ever approach the ultimate uses of the physicist's testimony to these questions.

It should be said : 2. Almost every fact brought forward by Dr. Clarke goes to illustrate the exact opposite of his almost every conclusion in respect to the effect of *mental* labor upon the female physique. With the serene, not to say dogmatic conviction of the physician whose own patients represent the world to him, he has copied for us from his note-books a series of cases exemplifying the remarkable unanimity with which girls, *after* leaving school, break down in health. Overlooking the blunder which he made about the student from Vassar College, which has been so carefully pointed out by Colonel Higginson (I refer to Dr. Clarke's implicit and unhesitating acceptance and publication of statements made by the student, which the faculty of the college have since altogether denied) ; not pausing to discuss the spirit which grasps at uninvestigated testimony like this, — run the eye over his illustrations, and what have we ?

With an affluent accompaniment of office detail so evidently necessary to the public discussion of an educational topic, and so unlikely to attract a purely irrelevant and unworthy attention to the circulation of the essay that one cannot fail to note the author's generosity in this particular, he calls our consideration to his list of cases, arguing detachedly, by the way, and ingeniously constructing for our benefit very much such a syllogism as this.

*Sumption.* — All women ought to be incapable of sustained activity.

*Subsumption.* — Some women whom I have known are incapable of sustained activity. Miss X. became an invalid soon after leaving school. Miss Y. was injured by gymnastic exercises, fell under my care, and will never be well. Miss Z. became an invalid soon after leaving school, and being for some time under my treatment was sent to an insane asylum.

Therefore,

Conclusion : All women are incapable of sustained activity, but proved especially incapable of sustained brain activity ; and, since it would cost Harvard College several millions of dollars to admit them, co-education is a chimera, and old maids a monstrosity at which physicians may sneer, and by which young women should take warning.

Or, to put it in another form, more compactly,

As long as girls are in school they are (with exceptions so rare that I have had great difficulty in finding them) in excellent health.

When girls leave school, they fall sick.

Therefore it is sustained study which injures girls.

Here, now, is the point of fair dispute. Why do girls so often become invalids within a few years after leaving school? The fact is a familiar one. We needed no Dr. Clarke come from their graves to tell us this. We are well accustomed to the sight of a fresh young girl, a close student, a fine achiever, "sustained" in mental application, and as healthy in body as she is vigorous and aspiring in brain, sinking, after a period of out-of-school life, into an aching, ailing, moping creature, aimless in the spirit and useless in the flesh for any of life's higher purposes, with which her young soul was filled and fired a little while ago.

"You may be well enough now. Wait till you are twenty four or five. That is the age when girls break down." This is the doleful prophecy of friends and physicians cast cold on the warm hopes of our hard-working, ambitious girls. " It is because you keep late hours, dance too much, eat indigestible food, or exercise too little," says the hygienist. "It is because you wear corsets, long skirts, and chignons," says the dress reformer. "It is because you are a woman. Here is a mystery!" says the dunce. "It is because you study too much," says Dr. Clarke.

Who of us has yet suggested and enforced the suggestion of another reason more simple and comprehensive than any of these, — more probable, perhaps, than any which could be found outside of the effects of female dress?

Women sick because they study? Does it not look a little more as if women were sick because they *stopped* studying?

Worn out by intellectual activity?

Let us suppose that they might be exhausted by the change from intellectual activity to intellectual inanition. Made invalids because they go to school from fourteen to eighteen? Let us conceive that they might be made invalids because they *left* school at eighteen! Let us draw upon our imagination to the extent of inquiring whether the nineteenth-century girl — intense, sensitive, and developing, like her age, nervously and fast — might not be made an invalid by the plunge from the " healing influences " of system-atic brain exertion to the broken, jagged life which awaits a girl whose " education is com-pleted." Made an invalid by exchanging the wholesome pursuit of sufficient and worthy aims for the unrelieved routine of a dependent domes-tic life, from which all aim has departed, or for the whirl of false excitements and falser contents which she calls society. Made an invalid by the abrupt slide from " thinking," as poor Lamb had it, " that life was going to be something," to the discovery that it has " unaccountably fallen from her before its time." Made an invalid by the sad and subtle process by which a girl is first inspired to the ideal of a life in which her per-sonal culture has as honest and honorable a part of her regard as (and as a part of) her personal usefulness ; and then is left to find out that per-sonal culture substantially stopped for her when she tied the ribbon of her seminary diploma.

Made an invalid by the prejudice that deprives
her of the stimulus which every human being
needs and finds in the pursuit of some one
especial avocation, and confines that avocation
for her to a marriage which she may never
effect, and which may never help the matter if
she does.    Made an invalid by the change from
doing something to doing nothing.    Made an
invalid by the difference between being happy
and being miserable.    Made an invalid, in short,
for *just the reasons* (in whatever manner, the
manner being a secondary point) *why a man
would be made an invalid* if subjected to the
woman's life when the woman's education is
over.    That wretched, mistaken life, that nervous, emotive, aimless, and exhausting life which
women assume at the end of their school career
would have killed Dr. Clarke, had it been his
lot, quite too soon for his years and experience
to have matured into the writing of " Sex in
Education."

Girls know what I mean.    Women who work
for women have some chance to read the mind

of women on such points. We could produce our own note-book over against the physician's, and the contents of it would be pitiful to see.

The sense of perplexed disappointment, of baffled intelligence, of unoccupied powers, of blunted aspirations, which run through the con- fidences of girls "left school," is enough to create any illness which nervous wear and misery can create. And the physician should be the first man to recognize this fact, — not the man to ignore or discredit it ; not the man to use his professional culture to the neglect of any obvious appeal to his professional candor ; not the man to veil within a few slippery flat- teries a wilful ignorance or an unmanly sneer.

Admitting what must be in justice said of " Sex in Education," — that its author's pro- fessional status demanded for his opinions, if expressed in the proper way and in the proper places, at least an intelligent hearing ; and that he has called attention to some evils in the training of very young girls which require, whether by his means or by some other, a

remedy ; and that he has made a sincere endeavor to point out these real and other imaginary evils in a manner good, at least in his own
eyes, — the sneer remains.[1]   By it women will
remember him when the work which he undertook to do shall be long forgotten.   Through it
the whole character of that work is vitiated and
its influence marred.   For it we may yet be
grateful, after all.

[1] Any reader of the essay will recall its flings at women
who, either from subjective preference or objective pressure,
are debarred from marriage and maternity.   These flings are
too disagreeable for pleasant quotation.

# VIII.

Dr. Clarke's book on "Sex in Education" should be read deliberately, thoughtfully, and in a spirit of fairness, which seeks only to know the real facts in the matter, and not to find arguments for or against any special theory, system, or hobby. Dr. Clarke is an eminent physician. All forms of disease are not only familiar to him, but are forced upon his attention: of course he sees the dark side of life, and judges accordingly. His picture of the condition of women is a terrible one, calculated to excite deep anxiety in parents, and in young women themselves: he sees in the future, if the present system of education is continued, only increasing invalidism, partial development, deformity, and the eventual failure of the American race. This alarming condition of affairs he attributes to various causes; and among the most powerful of these causes he reckons the common system of continuous education for girls. He calls it the boy's method, and means by it not any special curriculum of study, or any share in out-of-doors masculine plays or employments, but simply regular study for five or six days of every week. This, he thinks, is so grave an error, so absolutely criminal a course, that he has given to the world this book of warning, to stay, if he can, this evil; to save, if he can, American girls, to enable them to become mothers; for, he says, "if these causes of evil — persistent education chief among them — should continue for the next half century, and increase in the same ratio as they have for the last fifty years, it requires no prophet to foretell that the wives who are to be mothers in our republic must be drawn from transatlantic homes. The sons of the New World will have to react, on a magnificent scale, the old story of unwived Rome and the Sabines."

It is not education for women to which Dr.

Clarke objects. He repeats emphatically that they have a right to the best education and the finest culture. He does not doubt their intellectual ability ; but the essential thing in a good education is complete development, so that "boys may become men, and girls women, and both have a fair chance to do and become their best." Dr. Clarke's point is that the sustained regularity of study which benefits a boy inevitably harms a girl, prevents her from doing or becoming her best, and in a frightfully large proportion of cases actually ruins her health, and makes it impossible for her to nourish, and too often impossible for her to bear, children. This danger he discusses fully, and, as he says, with great plainness of speech, and without ambiguity of language or euphemism of expression. The peril seems to him imminent, and he cries aloud from his watch-tower of science and experience, and his cry will be heard and heeded by thousands. But there are other cries to be heard and heeded ; there are other watchmen who do not sleep at their posts, and who see brighter scenes burdensome clothes, not tight but cumbersome masses of their own or false hair on the head, that should be cool and free ; they eat unwholesome food ; dance at hot parties ; saunter along the pavements, with arms *à la mode;* go to dancing school and skating parties without the faintest regard to physiology or to the plain rules of health ; have music lessons and masters ; and in too many cases lead a life of reckless waste that it makes a grown person breathless to think of. No wonder they break down, no wonder they have all those miserable polysyllabic diseases that decently trained women never heard of ; but we believe that the class who have these diseases because of "sustained regularity" in study is so small that it should hardly be reckoned in the account, but should be treated as exceptional, like the blind or the physically deformed. It is almost impossible for even a physician to discover in the case of young invalids how much really hard and injurious study has been done. The imprudences, wilful or ignorant, of girls, are innumerable, and only when driven to the last extreme will they confess them.  If the evil resulting from bad diet, late and irregular hours, improper clothing, exposure to cold and dampness, hereditary weakness, and exciting reading, could be eliminated, we believe there would be no difficulty whatever in raising a generation of strong and noble girls under the system of "sustained regularity" of study.

There is something to be said from the side of health.  All women are not sick, and the experience of health teaches that girls and boys should have a very large margin for repair of waste and for growth,—girls, perhaps, a larger margin than boys, although we are by no means sure of that.  Nature is a wise worker, and distributes the repair and growth wherever it is needed, to the dual organism of the boy or to the tripartite one of the girl.  With simple, healthful habits of life, with proper diet, abundant sleep, plenty of sunshine and play, and moderate, regular study, in school or out, girls, unless they inherited some disease, would stand a fair chance for health, strength, and development as women.

dren between ten and sixteen were not allowed to serve in shops ; if no woman under twenty were allowed to teach in a public school ; if girls were taught obedience and truth-telling, and if mothers were wisely anxious,—that is Dr. Clarke's expression, and goes to the root of the matter, — wisely anxious about their daughters, caring for their health more than for their appearance, for their permanent good more than their present indulgence, looking after their reading and their pleasures, guarding them from imprudence and making them take care of their own health, there would be no trouble about regular study.    The same causes that dry up the youth and strength of young girls break down older ones, — constant excitement and no real rest ; social excitement at parties ; passionate excitement at operas and theatres ; emotional excitement over highly wrought novels and philanthropic work ; one following close on the other, and all accompanied by bodily fatigue and endless hurry.    It is a sad life to look at, in spite of the seeming beauty of the garments of art, culture, and charity which it wears. If Dr. Clarke's warning will waken people to their danger, and make them lead simpler and easier lives ; if he can make them follow the plainest rules of health ; if he can do any thing toward keeping girls girls, instead of having them forced, when they are hardly in their teens, into diminutive fashionable women, with a smattering of forty studies and a knowledge of none, — he will be indeed a Good Physician, and his aim will be won without taking girls out of school or interfering with their regular work, without even discussing the question of co-education. . . .

The accounts of the training of German girls given in the last chapter bear out these views. To be sure, most of the German girls leave school young, at about fifteen, and have lessons at home. We know nothing of the regularity, strictness, or requirements of these lessons or lectures ; but we do know the work is regular, and not periodical, for girls in average health, and the health is taken care of. There is an established kind of tradition, as there is in many

families in this country, in regard to the regimen
for girls.   Cold and exposure are avoided ; school-
girls never ride and never go to parties ; and, even
when school-days are over, girls do not go to
parties during the time when Dr. Clarke thinks
they ought not to go to school.   Dr. Hagen
writes : " The health of the German girls is com-
monly good, except in the higher classes in the
great capitals, where the same obnoxious agencies
are to be found in Germany as in the whole world.
But here also there is a very strong exception, or,
better, a difference between America and Germany, as German girls are never accustomed to
the free manners and modes of life of American
girls.   As a rule, in Germany *the " mother directs
the manner of living of the daughter entirely."*
The italics are ours.   Dr. Clarke adds to this
that " pleasant recreation for children of both
sexes, and abundance of it, is provided for them
all over Germany, — is regarded as necessity for
them, — is made a part of their daily life ; but
then it is open air, oxygen-surrounding, blood-
making, health-giving, innocent recreation, — not

gas, furnaces, low necks, spinal trails, — the civilized representatives of caudal appendages, — and late hours."

We repeat that Dr. Clarke does not oppose the education of women : he only opposes the present method of education. He says distinctly : Let us remember that physiology confirms the hope of the race by asserting that the loftiest heights of intellectual and spiritual vision and force are free to each sex, and accessible by each ; but adds that each must climb in its own way, and accept its own limitations, and, when this is done, promises that each will find the doing of it not to weaken or diminish, but to develop power. His book is written with force and with genuine earnestness and feeling, is full of valuable instruction, and is both useful and suggestive to those who will agree with the author, — to those who oppose him, and to those like ourselves who sympathize fully with his aim, but who think that he has laid the emphasis of blame wrongly. — *Boston Daily Advertiser.*

## IX.

### BY M. B. JACKSON.

In this little book, which has attracted much attention, there are many excellent things ; and we thank Dr. Clarke for having written it, not so much for what it contains as for the attention it has drawn to the subject of which it treats. Coming as it does from a physician, who stands so high in the profession, and who is so much esteemed in social life, it naturally attracts the attention of many who are thinking upon the subject of co-education.  But we regret to find that one who should be informed of the views of the prominent advocates of co-education should permit himself to talk of their wishing to make women as nearly as possible like men, and of women as wishing to become like men, and despising those differences in themselves which distinguish the sexes, when in fact these are the

opprobriums of their opponents instead of arguments to defeat the cause. On page 18 he says:

"It is said that Elina Carnaro, the accom-
plished professor of six languages, whose statue
adorns and honors Padua, was educated like a
boy. This means that she was initiated into and
mastered the studies that were considered to be
the peculiar dower of men. It does not mean
that her life was a man's life, her way of study a
man's way of study, or that in acquiring six
languages she ignored her own organization."

How the Doctor got this interpretation of
what is meant by Elina Carnaro's being educated like a boy he does not inform us, but no
woman would have thought that her life was
a man's life, her way of study a man's way of
study, or that in acquiring six languages she
would ignore her own organization. What women are now struggling for is not to be like
men, not to get their education by the same
mental processes as men, but to have the same
opportunities to use in a woman's way, and to
make the most of them in the methods their

course for women, assuming that he is a better judge of what they can bear than they are themselves, and assuming that if allowed to decide for themselves what they could bear they would destroy themselves by excessive study! This is not exactly consistent with his admission of their intellectual equality with men; but women have been long accustomed to being told that they are the intellectual peers of men, and, in the next breath, that they do not know what is best for them, and that men are their natural protectors and supporters, and that they should defer all matters relating to their welfare to the better judgment of men, who will take all the trouble of such decisions from them and settle such questions in the way that will promote their greatest happiness! When the time comes that men have so far mastered the plan of the universe as to perceive that the Creator has endowed each class of animals with its own peculiar method of defence, and capable of choosing the way of life most in harmony with its nature, and that man, the highest in the grade of created beings, is also endowed with the power of seeing what will best conserve his interest, and that he has not made one-half of the race incapable of choosing wisely, and therefore dependent upon the other half for this information a great step will be taken in the right direction, and equal freedom of action being secured by the removal of all laws and customs that limit women to narrower bounds than men will give an opportunity to decide the question of what women can do and will do, when allowed free scope for all their powers.

The Doctor talks as if the Creator had made man so perfectly that, without any special care on his part, his whole nature would naturally develop into a perfect and healthy human being, prepared to fulfil all objects of his creation ; but that He made woman so imperfectly that her organism would not naturally develop into a perfectly healthy woman, fitted to fulfil the high objects of her creation, unless men took charge of her and directed what she must do and how she must live.

Is not this impugning the wisdom of the Creator in assuming that He left a being on whom the welfare of the race greatly depends to the poor care of erring mortals, instead of creating her as He has man, so that she would naturally grow into a perfect woman from the very nature of her constitution? We take no issue with the Doctor in regard to the host of ills that women are suffering from at this time in America; but they are certainly not to be charged to co-education, for that has been so little tried that no conclusions can as yet be drawn from it.

So far as our observation goes, the number of invalid women is greater in the class of fashionable women than in any other; and they surely do not overtax their brains in studies that compose the college curriculum. The want of some noble and engrossing subject of thought and action is, in our opinion, a much more frequent cause of ill-health than over-study, and next to that, if not taking precedence of it, is the manner in which women are clothed. The corsets that confine the waists and abdomen as if in a vice, preventing the action of the muscles and pressing down the contents of the abdomen, so as to displace important organs ; the great weight of skirts hanging on the abdominal muscles ; the long skirts that fetter the limbs and prevent a natural movement of them ; the thin boots that expose the feet to cold and damp ; the high heels that throw the body out of the perpendicular line, so that a constant strain is imposed on the muscles to keep the balance, — these are prolific causes of invalidism. The late hours and continued excitements of parties and balls, the great exposure to cold from changing the warm dresses worn in winter for the thin party dresses for evening, combined with the unwholesome diet on such occasions, complete the destruction of health, never robust on account of the failure to give girls the out-of-door active exercises which boys enjoy, while as yet there is no physiological reason for their being shut up in the house, or only taken out to walk dressed so finely that play and exercise are out of the question.

There is still another case, which to my mind is as clear as the overtaxing of brains is to Dr.

Clarke's ; and that is the necessity for women to go to physicians of the male sex when they need advice for their peculiar diseases. The medical colleges, refusing admission to women, kept them out of the regular avenues for acquiring a medical education, and consequently the number of educated women physicians was so small that they could scarcely be mentioned as treating the diseases of women ; and the result has been that for a long period women have been treated by men who, having no corresponding organs, could not possibly understand their diseases, and they have been left uncured, only palliated, and often made worse by this great error. When women are permitted to add the light of science and art to their personal experiences and similar organizations, we may look for a healthier race of women.

On page 54 he says : —

" This growing period or formative epoch extends from birth to the age of twenty or twenty-five years. Its duration is shorter for a girl than for a boy. She ripens quicker than he. In the four years from fourteen to eighteen, she accomplishes an amount of cell change and growth which Nature does not require of a boy in less than twice that number of years. It is obvious that, to secure the best kind of growth during this period and the best development at the end of it, the waste of tissue produced by study, work, and fashion must not be so great that repair will only equal it. It is equally obvious that a girl, upon whom Nature for a limited period and for a definite purpose imposes so great a physiological task, will not have as much power left for the tasks of the school as the boy, of whom Nature requires less at the corresponding epoch. A margin must be left for growth. The repair must be greater and better than the waste."

Did it not occur to the Doctor's mind that "Nature," or the Creator, in making woman, took this state of things into account, and provided for it, by supplying the female organism at this period with a power of more rapid cell growth to meet this want, and that this same power would be needed by the woman when the great drain of reproducing the race was made upon her system ? If such had not been the case, women would succumb at once to the great waste necessitated by child-bearing, and no mother would live to have a second child. But the Infinite Father knew how to make woman, so that under ordinary circumstances she could go on with her usual activities, and bear children without injury to her health, and often with an improvement of it. For, of our healthy women at sixty or seventy years of age, nearly all have been mothers, and most of them have had large families.

When the Doctor says, "Two considerations deserve to be mentioned in this connection : one is, that no organ or function in plant, animal, or human kind, can be properly regarded as a disability or source of weakness," — he states a well-known fact ; but when he attempts to show that one of the functions of woman is a great disability, and necessarily incapacitates her from the performance of usual duties two or three days out of every thirty, he directly contradicts his first statement. Healthy women are able to go on with their usual avocations at these times, and only feeble or sickly ones require the rest he speaks of. Those girls whose physical train-ing has been such as to give them strong bodies develop naturally and without suffering, just as boys do, and find no necessity for dropping all mental and physical labor two days in every month. Neither men nor women can overtax for a long time their mental or physical natures, and remain well. There is one law for both, and it is inflexible ; but is it necessary for man to ask woman, or woman man, what either can bear without injury ? Must not each be a law unto himself ? Let women study physiology and thoroughly understand their own bodies, and they can be trusted to take care of them. Why the Doctor supposes it necessary to co-education that women should study like men, or should be obliged to stand for recitations, I cannot imagine. Are the rules of college inflexible, like the laws of the Medes and Persians ? or are they made for

K

the best good of the students ?  If a class sits during recitations, does it follow that their lessons will be less well learned ?  If a girl can get a lesson in an hour that requires a boy an hour and a half to learn, will it be necessary for her to study as many hours as the boy, to keep up with him ?  And does not every teacher of boys and girls know that girls, as a rule, take less time to commit their tasks than boys ?  By the Doctor's own showing, this is in analogy with the processes in their physical frames ; for he says, " In the four years, from fourteen to eighteen, she accomplishes an amount of physiological cell change and growth which Nature does not require of a boy in less than twice that number of years."  The trouble with the Doctor is, that he has a pet theory that women must not do mental or physical work during certain periods ; and so he attributes all disease in women to failure in securing this rest, whether it be want of development of the ovaries, hemorrhages, or disease of the brain !

But we would again thank him for his book,

which is so suggestive that thinking women cannot read it without seeing the necessity for reformation in many ways of the false ideas and customs regarding woman's training, dressing, and living ; and, having their attention called to them, it is to be hoped they will make an earnest effort to improve upon them.

## X.

### BY PROFESSOR BASCOM.

THE following is an extract from a paper read at the recent Massachusetts Teachers' Convention in Worcester : —

To the present point of composition in this paper, I had not had the opportunity of a full perusal of Dr. Clarke's work, entitled " Sex in Education." I wish, therefore, to add a few things directly bearing on it. The consideration chiefly dwelt on by Dr. Clarke, that of periodicity and continuity, respectively, in sexual development, is one of great importance, demanding earnest and thorough attention. His work is able, candid, and fair. It is not, however, fair in its actual practical bearing on co-education. The impression is made by it that it presses peculiarly upon this point, and that its general conclusions, if admitted, are well-nigh fatal to it. This is not true, and is hardly the author's meaning.

In the first place, the general debility of women, be it greater or less, is not due to co-education in higher knowledge ; for such an education has not existed among us to a degree sufficient perceptibly to affect the general constitution. It is due to an ignorance and inattention to physiological law that have characterized all our action in business, social, and educational relations, in the former even more than in the latter. Separate training, as that at Mt. Holyoke, has been as deeply affected by it as joint education, like that at Oberlin. The point raised by Dr. Clarke bears on all our action, not pre-eminently on one part of it, and that hitherto a most insignificant part, the portion expressed in conjoint higher education. To give the hygienic considerations involved this peculiar and limited application is illogical and unfair. The reform called for will effect this method in common with a hundred other things. If the conclusions already reached by us in this paper are to be altered by the considerations presented by Dr. Clarke, it must be by showing that co-education is inconsistent with a proper regard of the hygienic rules involved in sexual development. The present debility of women goes for nothing in the argument. This debility, as due in given cases to a false training, goes for nothing, since our inattention has been general, and covers this field with many another. We might as well argue against social inter-course, since this, even oftener than lessons, has been the provocation to excess. The only real question, then, between Dr. Clarke and co-education is this : Can co-education be so altered as to respect, in both sexes, the laws of development ? He himself practically con-cedes that it can be. He only objects finally and peremptorily to identical co-education ; that is, to precisely the same tasks, at all times, for all parties. To this we also object, as unfitted for the best development of boys and girls alike. The active and the inert, the bright and the dull, cannot be harnessed together without loss on one side or the other. Our education, in the interest of boys as well as of girls, calls for more elasticity, less pressure, more variable and proportionate stimulus. Construct a method good for boys of all kinds, pliant to their wants, keeping up with the best, and falling back to the poorest, and we shall have a system sufficiently flexible to include girls, under their own law of development.

Indeed, the rigidity of college courses is precisely that which needs modification ; and, if this is to come with co-education, so much the better for the joint discipline. The average girl, carrying weight as she does in the laws of her constitution, is not as far off from the average boy as the stupid boy from the quick-witted one. Unite these two well in one system, and that system will have play enough to embrace girls also advantageously. Our present difficulties are due to bad education, not to co-education ; to an ignorance of the laws of hygiene, not to a knowledge of these and their witting violation. Educate women more thoroughly, and they will be more cognizant and observant of these conditions of success. As things now are, they owe their disease to their ignorance : they are not weak because they are wise, but weak because they are not wise.

The critical period, according to Dr. Clarke, is found between the ages of fourteen and eighteen. This is a period for the most part prior, and may to advantage be always prior, to that given to higher education, and one covered by the kind and accommodating provisions of home. I have not the slightest doubt that, if the general temper that is encouraged by Dr. Clarke's essay, were left to shape a sexual curriculum for women, it would issue in a feeble intellectual mood, a proportionate diversion of time, strength, and interest to society, — sure to absorb unoccupied powers, heedless and headstrong in its use of them, — and thus ultimately in strengthening the very evil warred with. Society is more to be dreaded than education. On the other hand, devote attention to a complete elastic common curriculum, and the tastes will be elevated, the judgment sobered, the conditions of success made more apparent, and ultimately that breadth and strength of character reached which are sure to express themselves in a wise mastery of natural law. If we are bound to have a thoroughly flexible and fit discipline for boys, in reaching it we shall also furnish appropriate conditions for girls, and all the reasons for co-education urged by us will apply in full force. The transition from a rigid to a pliant method will necessarily take place slowly ; but we do well to remember that the cast-iron mode is as firmly wrought into separate as into conjoint education, and constitutes no ground of choice between them. Both are to be reformed, both are capable of reform, and in the interests of all parties. Dr. Clarke's criticism is destructive, not constructive. Let him undertake to build up a curriculum, and the advantage will at once pass to his opponents.

8

# XI.

## BY ABBY W. MAY.

*[Extract from Annual Report of Committee on Work of the New England Women's Club, read May 31, 1873.]*

OUR programme for the year just closed occupied itself with the question of women's fitness for entering practical life, presented from several points of view. At our first meeting, Miss Kellogg, in an able manner, set before us the views of several of the most eminent scientific men on the question of the relative capacity of women for the highest education. The extracts Miss Kellogg gave proved that there is a good deal of difference of opinion among authorities ; but, whatever may be the conclusion to-day of one or another man, the great desideratum is that the matter should be frankly discussed. Truth will inevitably result sooner or later ; and that is what we chiefly desire, even when the lesson of patience is bitterly hard. This valuable *ré-sumé* of the opinions of others was followed by a highly interesting paper from Dr. Edward H. Clarke, upon the health of women, as affecting steady, persistent mental application. Dr. Clarke — the skilful physician, the jealous guardian of health, to whose notice comes daily most distressing knowledge of the suffering caused by a lack of it, especially among New England women — made a strong plea for saving women from the over-pressure and false methods of living, under which so many men, as well as women, break down. The sad fact of great physical weakness among our women is beyond dispute. In that respect, there is no room for difference of opinion; though we thought Dr. Clarke did not sufficiently recognize the gain which has been made in some respects within the last few years. But the discussion which followed the paper showed that the majority could not agree with Dr. Clarke, in charging much of the misery upon high education or the co-education of the sexes. There are many

very best there is, because of danger to a woman's body, — a danger different in its nature from that which men so often find in unwise mental effort? No one would plead for folly, as applied to the training of either sex; but that many women are feeble seems a poor reason for depriving those who are strong of any advantage that the world can afford them. Does he want it? is the question we ask in relation to men. Does she want it? would seem to be the only fair one to ask of the other sex. For both sexes, lack of health must often be practically an insurmountable barrier. Why cannot all interested in this question unite in holding up a high standard of health, in themselves and for others, since no other obstacle can long prevent women from having all the educational advantages they can use.

## XII.

### BY MARIA A. ELMORE.

DR. CLARKE talks as though women in every thing but college life had perfect liberty to change at will their position from the erect to the reclining; as though nothing else required four weeks' labor in a month ; as though a regular, sustained, and uninterrupted course of work was something of which they have never had any experience ; and as though identical education of the sexes was the only regimen that ignored the periodic tides and reproductive apparatus of their organization.

We would like to have Dr. Clarke inform us what regimen there is that does not ignore them ?

While but very few women are called by a chapel-bell to a standing prayer, thousands and tens of thousands in America are called by the bell of "that university, which has a water-wheel at the bottom," to all-day standing tasks at the noisy loom, and this followed from half-past six in the morning till half-past six at night, with the intermission only of half, three-quarters, or the whole of an hour at noon, throughout every working-day in the year.

Has Dr. Clarke written a book on "Sex in Manufacturing Establishments"? If he hasn't, he ought to.

Women stand behind the counter, obliged to be at their post just such a time every morning, and to wait on customers, if need be, the livelong day. Are they excused from work every fourth week? Can they sit, stand, or recline at their pleasure? Are they exempted from tending to the wants of their employers' patrons because they feel indisposed? Nay, in many instances are they not required to be on their feet all the time, even when there are no customers?

Has Dr. Clarke written a book on "Sex in Clerkships"?

Women have, year out and year in, busily plied

the needle in tailors' and dressmakers' shops, having no opportunity to change at will their position from the sitting to the standing, walking, or reclining.

Has Dr. Clarke written a book on " Sex in Workshops," or " Sex in Sewing " ?

School-teachers are expected to be in their school-rooms promptly on the hour every school-day in the year, ready to discharge their duties to their pupils. Where is the school-board that ever allowed its female teachers to take a week's vacation every month ? Where is that man who would have a young woman teach in his ward or neighborhood who should make application to him in this wise : " Sir, I am very desirous of becoming a teacher. I want a school, and will do all in my power to bring it to a standard of high moral excellence and worth. But I must tell you that I cannot teach for four consecutive weeks. I can teach only three weeks at a time : the fourth I must have to myself. Mighty and powerful demands are then made upon my constitution, and it requires all the strength and energy I can command to meet them. To attempt at such times to manage and instruct an unruly and rollicking set of young urchins would derange the tides of my organization, divert blood from the reproductive apparatus to my head, and consequently add to my piety at the expense of my blood."

Women teach school under a regimen that pays no more regard to their bodily organism than to that of men. Yet in the face of this fact Dr. Clarke tells us it is a sin under such a regimen to attend school as a pupil! Are the duties and responsibilities of a pupil so much more arduous and exacting than those of a teacher that a much more favorable regimen must be prescribed for the former than for the latter?

Imagine Miss Applicant, in quest of a situation to do housework, addressing mistress of the house as follows : "You know, my dear woman, that public opinion and sentiment have imposed upon girls a boy's regimen ; that is, that girls who go out to work are expected to work every day of the month, just as boys do. Now this is altogether wrong and contrary to the laws of

8* L

nature. It is grounded on the supposition that sustained regularity of action may be as safely required of a girl as a boy ; that there is no physical necessity for periodically relieving her from standing, walking, cooking, or baking ; that the striking of the clock may call her as well as him to a daily morning walk with the baby, with standing work at the end of it, regardless of the danger that such exercise, by deranging the tide of her organization, may add to her piety at the expense of her blood ; that she may bother her brain over bread, pies, cake, preserves, condiments, and the like, with equal and sustained force on every day of the month, thus diverting blood from the reproductive apparatus to the head ; in short, that she, like her brother, develops health, strength, blood, and nerve by a regular, uninterrupted, and sustained course of work. All this is not justified either by experience or physiology. Girls lose all these by doing housework all the time. By requiring a girl to perform the same round of duties every day of the month, you impose upon her a regi-

men which ignores the periodical tides and reproductive apparatus of her organization. Allow me
to tell you, dear madame, that work every fourth
week the same as the other three, lack of privi-
lege to change her position when she needs
change, persistent exercise and constant labor,
which you say any girl who works in your household will be subjected to, are wicked. It will do
very well for a *boy;* it will toughen and make a
man of him; but it can be only prejudicial to a
girl. Surely, ma'am, you can't expect girls to
work every week: they would become agenes
under such a regimen as that."

Would she be likely to secure the situation?
Is it the prerogative of those who go out to
housework, or who perform any kind of service
or labor, to suspend work every fourth week?
Are not all women expected to do the bidding of
their employers, the same as men, however great
their disinclination?

Does that regimen which men are ever pre-
scribing for woman, namely, marriage, grant her
one week's cessation from labor out of every

four ? Can a mother, when weary and over-
tasked, relinquish the work and care of her
family, and engage her thoughts upon nothing
save that of her own physical weaknesses, and
how to relieve them ?

No, women may work in the factory, in the
store, in the workshop, in the field, in the dining-
saloon, at the wash-tub, at the ironing-table, at
the sewing-machine, — do all these things, and
many more equally hard, from Monday morning
till Saturday night every week in the year ; may
wear their lives out toiling for their children,
and doing the work for their families that their
husbands ought to do, and nobody raises the arm
of opposition ; but just now, because there is a
possibility and even probability that in matters
of education women will be as honorably treated
as men, lo ! Dr. Clarke comes forth and tells us
it ought not to be so, because, forsooth, the periodical tides and reproductive apparatus of her
organization will be ignored !

If there are any spheres of labor or of action
that have with earnest solicitude more carefully

and faithfully looked after the health of the girls and women who every day repair within their walls than have many of our seminaries of learning, we have yet to learn the fact.

So long as men are willing that women should do all or any of the things herein specified, beside the thousand and one things to which we have no space to allude ; so long as men are willing she should enter marriage, a regimen which imposes more duties, responsibilities, trials, burdens, cares, and sorrows than any other can, which taxes health, strength, blood, and nerve infinitely more than any thing else she can ever do ; so long as they are willing that she should endure the wear and tear of wifehood and motherhood, the severest and most trying ordeals through which human beings are ever called to pass, and, in comparison to the burdens which it inflicts upon her physical organization, all others are of a straw's weight ; so long as men are willing that woman should act, work, labor, earn her living in these various capacities, not one of which gives her more opportunity to favor herself than it gives man, is it not insulting for a physician to single out one individual phase of action, and declare that it is a sin for woman to share equally with man in the advantages it affords, because it don't pay so much attention to the subject of catamenia as he thinks it ought?

Will Dr. Clarke please tell us why colleges, or places of learning of any kind, should be denied to woman on the ground that an insufficient amount of deference is given to her physiological nature, any more than other institutions which overlook it entirely?

## XIII.

### BY A. C. GARLAND.

A VERY flattering notice of the volume bearing the title " Sex in Education" having appeared in the "Journal," one "ambitious woman," who is not "fretting under the restraints which nature imposes," but those arbitrary and unjust social laws which have grown out of a false, partial, and superficial view of nature's laws, and who is not "meditating the dangerous experiment of making herself a man," but has long claimed for herself and other women the right of deciding what constitutes womanhood, feels moved to reply.

Not having read the book in question, we shall simply attack the position of its admirer. We find, first, a complaint that the "subject" of woman's co-education with man "has been treated as a matter purely of moral claim, not of natural capacity," by many. Those who have claimed equal educational advantages for women as a right have in nearly if not all cases done so because of the following unanswerable reasons : While women are taxed for the support of higher schools of instruction, they have a moral claim on such institutions for the equal education of both sexes. The statement of any author, that "experience and careful observation have proved that the higher education of women has been detrimental to their health, is simply an assumption of his own, which can be met by as determined and well-proven statements on the other side. The fact is, that we cannot absolutely settle the limits of woman's strength and endurance by any experiments made and recorded so imperfectly as they must be at a time like the present, when the majority of women who are educating themselves thoroughly in public colleges are doing so at the cost of home comforts, and under a severe pressure resulting from poverty. There was a time in the history of New England when the great majority of young men who were studying for the Christian ministry were in such poor health that sanctity and an earnest purpose came to be associated in almost every person's mind with a body just ready to fall a victim to any disease, a cadaverous or "spiritual" face, and a thin and wasted hand. Why was this? Not because the simple preparation of study injured them, but because they could not afford the generous living and comfortable homes which the body requires for its development, and their necessities compelled them to work outside their studies, while their student enthusiasm led them to disregard many laws of health. For these same reasons many a woman to-day fails in her course, when so near the end that a few more years would land her in competence and congenial employment. The health of the young ladies in Vassar College — where the curriculum is quite as exhaustive and exhausting as the various special courses at Harvard, to say the least — is excellent, as statistics, not theories, show. In the early history of Oberlin, the pioneer in higher education of the sexes, we read the names of

But we insist upon it that no person who discusses the educational problem of the present day, with an argument "based on the postulate that woman finds her normal development in fulfilling the functions of wife and mother, and that any education which tends to unfit her for these highest offices is not a boon, but a curse," is worthy to be followed by just men or women. Men and women are "normally developed" when, and when only, they are rounded and broadened by culture of body, mind, and heart, into a symmetrical character. We have no more right to say that women shall be educated to be wives and mothers than that men shall be educated to be husbands and fathers ; and no more right to say that a woman is not fulfilling her "highest" office, who is laboring for the world in some other sphere than that of wifehood or motherhood, than we have to declare a man abnormally or imperfectly "developed" who has deemed it best to live his life unmarried. Until men are willing to discuss woman's education in the same way they do that of their own sex, on the broad healthfulness of student life for men or women, boys or girls, when the laws of health, namely, simple living, good food, abundant sleep, healthful clothing, and sufficient exercise in the open air, are known and observed. We will only add our wish that men would be as careful for the health of women in other respects as they claim to be in the matter of education ; and sum up all we would like to say on this vexed question in one sentence : That man or woman is best fitted for his or her special relations who is most thoroughly and harmoniously developed as an individual.

# TESTIMONY FROM COLLEGES.

———

Dr. Edward H. Clarke.

Dear Sir, — Having held the office of Resident Physician in Vassar College since the school opened, — September, 1865, — it seems to me that I have the right to make respectful but earnest protest against the implied strictures upon the hygienic teaching and practice of the institution, which I find in the history of " Miss D.," page 79 of " Sex in Education."

I take it that the aim of your book is to show parents and teachers the wrong they do women, and so the race, by their systematic overtaxing of the mental forces during the critical years of girlhood, when the reproductive function is asserting itself, and when every thing that would hinder its proper establishment should be carefully avoided.   In that aim I bid you God-speed;

and it is because I feel so strongly on that point, and have labored so zealously to make practical application of this physiological principle, that I regret that you should have taken as your most elaborately discussed and aggravated case one which so misrepresents the college that any person who is at all acquainted with its rules and management can hardly help having his confidence in the book shaken. He would naturally say, "This being so largely false, where can I be sure of finding the truth?"

Vassar College does not receive students under fifteen years of age, even for the first preparatory class (there is a two years' preparatory course). No student ever entered the freshman class at fourteen.

At the beginning of every collegiate year the students are carefully instructed regarding the precautions which are periodically necessary for them. They are positively forbidden to take gymnastics at all during the first two days of their period; and, if there is the least tendency toward menorrhagia, dysmenorrhœa, or other like irregularity, to forego those exercises entirely. They are also forbidden to ride on horseback then ; and, moreover, are strongly advised not to dance, nor *run* up and down stairs, nor do any thing else that gives sudden and successive (even though not violent) shocks to the trunk. They are encouraged to go out of doors for quiet walks, or drives, or boating, and to do whatever they can to steady the nervous irritation, and to help them to be patient with themselves through the almost inevitable excitement or depression that then supervenes.

That a student should faint again and again in the gymnasium, and still be pushed to continue her exercises there, is a statement that would not be made by any one who knows the *personal physical* care that is had here, not only by the Resident Physician, but by all the teachers. It is a statement that will be believed by none who has taken any pains to inform himself of the methods of training adopted by Vassar College.

It is possible that a student began here to

9                                   M

menstruate healthily, and ended her course a victim of dysmenorrhœa ; but does it give "a fair chance for the girls" to argue therefrom that the functional disturbance was the result of too severe or continued study ? Do you know that she pursued a healthful regimen in every other respect ? As an offset to this side of the story, I can give you a hundred cases in which dysmenorrhœa of long standing and aggravated character has been cured here,—cured mainly, as I believe, by patient persistence in the regular habits of mental and physical life that here obtain.

We do not attempt to cut down the work of each girl every fourth week, but we do mean so to regulate the work of the whole time that the end of no day shall find her overtaxed, even if that day has borne the added periodic burden. It is our aim so to combine opportunity for serious mental activity with physical training and individual freedom from tiresome restraint or hint of espionage, that vigor of head and heart and body will be the happy result. As a rule, we succeed ; the success varying of course with the stuff we have to work with.

The average age of the graduates of Vassar College is twenty-one and a half.

Too young, I grant you ; and we hope to improve on it as the years go, and knowledge, physiological and otherwise liberal, increases.

Eighteen is young enough for any woman to begin this course. At that age, with average endowment of mind and body, she pursues it with gladness and ends it with rejoicing, as can be proved by a goodly number of Vassar's alumnæ.

Hoping that your sense of justice will suggest methods by which the erroneous impressions that your book conveys concerning Vassar College may be, as far as possible, corrected,

I am, sir,

Respectfully yours,

ALIDA C. AVERY.

VASSAR COLLEGE, Poughkeepsie, N.Y.,
*Nov.* 4, 1873.

## ANTIOCH COLLEGE.

| Individual. | Year of Graduation. | Married or Single. | No. of Children. | Health. | Remarks. |
|---|---|---|---|---|---|
| 1 | 1857 | Married | 3 | Not living | Died 1874. |
| 2 | ,, | ,, | 1 | Good | Taught 11 years. Now in Indiana. |
| 3 | ,, | ,, | 2 | ,, | Has taught ever since graduating. Now in Ohio. |
| 4 | 1858 | ,, | 2 | Very good | Taught five years. Now in Ohio. |
| 5 | ,, | ,, | 6 | Good | Has taught school. Slight bronchial trouble. |
| 6 | 1859 | ,, | 3 | ,, | |
| 7 | ,, | ,, | 3 | Uncertain | Has taught school. |
| 8 | ,, | ,, | | Good | Taught thirteen years, till married in 1872. |
| 9 | ,, | ,, | 2 or 3 | | No recent intelligence. Health good as far as known. |
| 10 | 1860 | Single | | ,, | Taught some years. Now in England. |
| 11 | ,, | Married | 2 | ,, | Taught three years. |
| 12 | ,, | Single | | ,, | Has taught school. |
| 13 | ,, | ,, | | Very good | Physician in Missouri. |
| 14 | ,, | Married | 1 | ,, ,, | Has taught school. |
| 15 | ,, | Single | | ,, ,, | Constantly a teacher, except two years in Europe. |
| 16 | ,, | Married | | ,, ,, | Minister in Connecticut. Lately married. |
| 17 | 1861 | ,, | | Good | Taught three years. Journalist in Ohio. |
| 18 | ,, | ,, | 1 | | Has taught school. |
| 19 | 1862 | ,, | 1 | Not living | Died of hereditary consumption. |
| 20 | ,, | ,, | 1 | ,, ,, | |
| 21 | ,, | ,, | 1 | Good | |
| 22 | ,, | ,, | 2 | Very good | Resides in Ohio. |
| 23 | ,, | ,, | 2 | ,, ,, | Resides in Vermont. |
| 24 | ,, | ,, | 2 | ,, ,, | Resides in New York. |
| 25 | ,, | ,, | | Good | Lately married. |
| 26 | ,, | ,, | 3 | ,, | Has taught school. |
| 27 | 1863 | ,, | 2 | Very good | Taught four years, till married. |
| 28 | 1864 | Married | 3 | ,, ,, | Taught one year. |
| 29 | 1866 | ,, | | Not good | Troubled with scrofula, dating back earlier than her school days. Practises medicine in Missouri. |

| Individual. | Year of Graduation. | Married or Single. | No. of Children. | Health. | Remarks. |
|---|---|---|---|---|---|
| 30 | 1868 | Single | | Very good | Has just returned from three years in Europe, where she took long pedestrian journeys. |
| 31 | ,, | Married | 1 | Good | Has taught school and is teaching now. |
| 32 | ,, | ,, | 2 | ,, | Taught three years. |
| 33 | 1869 | Single | | ,, | Taught constantly and is teaching now. |
| 34 | 1870 | Married | | Not living | Died in 1871. |
| 35 | ,, | ,, | 1 | Good | Has taught school in Missouri. |
| 36 | ,, | ,, | 1 | ,, | Taught one year. |
| 37 | 1871 | Single | | Unknown | Came to college in delicate health, which improved while there. The youngest woman who ever graduated at Antioch. |
| 38 | 1872 | ,, | | Not living | Died 1873 of hereditary consumption. |
| 39 | ,, | ,, | | Fair | Teaching in Massachusetts. |
| 40 | 1873 | ,, | | Good | |
| 41 | ,, | ,, | | ,, | |

All the time I was at Antioch College I never heard of a young lady in the college requiring a physician's advice. Among the seven girls in my class I never remember an instance of illness: they were always at recitations, and always had their lessons. I spent four years at Antioch, — two at the theological school ; and I have been over ten years a settled pastor, and I never yet was absent from an engagement or suspended labor on account of sickness. When in Kansas, I spoke every day from the first of July to the fifth of November, besides travelling to my appointments each day, some days giving two lectures and preaching Sundays, making in all two hundred and five speeches, averaging more than an hour in length, and came home just as well as I went ; and this moment I am as well as ever, and could walk ten miles in a day with ease. To me such statements as Dr. Clarke's seem absurd, and contrary to everybody's experience. . . .

The ill-health of the women of our time is not due to study or regularity in study : it is due to the want of regularity, and want of aim and purpose, and want of discipline. If you should take the whole number of women in this country who have graduated from a regular college with men, and place them side by side with the same number of women who have not had that course of study, select them where you will, the college graduates will be stronger in mind and body, able to endure more and work harder than the others. This I am sure of, as I am acquainted with many of the somewhat small number of women graduates; and I know something of other women, having belonged to various female seminaries at different times. — *Rev. Olympia Brown.*

----

## MICHIGAN UNIVERSITY.

About eighty of the students are of the sex which some call "weaker," but which here, at any rate, is shown to be equal in endurance, in courage, in perseverance, in devotion to study, and in cheerful confidence, to the strong and stalwart men. The health of the women who are here now is in almost every instance excellent. I am assured by intelligent ladies in all the departments that there is not a single instance of sickness which has come from over-study, or from any cause connected with the routine of the college life. In one or two cases, the inconvenience of a weak constitution, of weak eyes and sensitive nerves, has been felt; and one of the most vigorous of the sisters has been confined to her chamber for some weeks by a sprained ankle. But it is the unanimous testimony, as I learn, of the ladies who are studying law, and medicine, and science, and the arts, in the class-rooms, and lecture-rooms, and library, and laboratory, that their health was never better, that they have had no attacks of malady, and that they ask for no indulgence on account of their sex. Most of them, indeed, are out of their teens, and beyond the age to which the warnings of Dr. Clarke's book apply. But, of the twenty or more whom I personally know, not one complains; and they look to be in better health than the average of young women.

Some say that it is too soon to pronounce upon the success of the experiment of co-education here; but, if the opinion of the women themselves, and of the teachers who teach them, is to be accepted, the experiment in the present season is as successful physically as it is intellectually. The women are as strong and hearty to all appearance, and have not found their sex an obstacle to their activity and comfort in study. — *Rev. C. H. Brigham, in Christian Register.*

———

## LOMBARD UNIVERSITY.

THE testimony from Lombard University, Galesburg, Illinois, is as follows : —

The whole number of graduates is sixty-nine men and forty-five women, of whom twenty-eight of the women have graduated during the last six years. There have been no permanent invalids. Nine men and three women have died. Twenty of the women have married, eleven of whom are mothers. The president, who had been here eighteen years, thinks — and, so far as I know, his opinion is the opinion of all who have been connected with the institution — that the women are as healthy as the men. It frequently happens that girls improve in health after coming here ; and I have heard two or three of them

9*

say, after graduating and returning home, that they should be stronger if they could come back and again have regular work and a definite aim.

---

### OBERLIN.

From Oberlin, Professor Fairchild says : —

A breaking down in health does not appear to be more frequent with women than with men. We have not observed a more frequent interruption of study on this account, nor do our statistics show a greater draft upon the vital forces in the case of those who have completed the full college course. Out of eighty-four who have graduated since 1841, seven have died, a proportion of one in twelve. Of three hundred and sixty-eight young men who have graduated in the same time, thirty-four are dead, or a little more than one in eleven. Of these thirty-four young men, six fell in the war ; and, leaving out those, the proportion of deaths remains one in thirteen. Taking the whole number of graduates, omitting the theological department, we find the proportion of deaths one in nine and a half; of ladies, one in twelve, and this in spite of the lower average expectation of life for women, as indicated in Life Insurance Tables.

Cambridge: Press of John Wilson and Son.

# *American Women: Images and Realities*
## An Arno Press Collection

[Adams, Charles F., editor]. **Correspondence between John Adams and Mercy Warren Relating to Her "History of the American Revolution," July-August, 1807.** With a new appendix of specimen pages from the **"History."** 1878.

[Arling], Emanie Sachs. **"The Terrible Siren": Victoria Woodhull, (1838-1927).** 1928.

Beard, Mary Ritter. **Woman's Work in Municipalities.** 1915.

Blanc, Madame [Marie Therese de Solms]. **The Condition of Woman in the United States.** 1895.

Bradford, Gamaliel. **Wives.** 1925.

Branagan, Thomas. **The Excellency of the Female Character Vindicated.** 1808.

Breckinridge, Sophonisba P. **Women in the Twentieth Century.** 1933.

Campbell, Helen. **Women Wage-Earners.** 1893.

Coolidge, Mary Roberts. **Why Women Are So.** 1912.

Dall, Caroline H. **The College, the Market, and the Court.** 1867.

[D'Arusmont], Frances Wright. **Life, Letters and Lectures: 1834, 1844.** 1972.

Davis, Almond H. **The Female Preacher, or Memoir of Salome Lincoln.** 1843.

Ellington, George. **The Women of New York.** 1869.

Farnham, Eliza W[oodson]. **Life in Prairie Land.** 1846.

Gage, Matilda Joslyn. **Woman, Church and State.** [1900].

Gilman, Charlotte Perkins. **The Living of Charlotte Perkins Gilman.** 1935.

Groves, Ernest R. **The American Woman.** 1944.

Hale, [Sarah J.] **Manners; or, Happy Homes and Good Society All the Year Round.** 1868.

Higginson, Thomas Wentworth. **Women and the Alphabet.** 1900.

Howe, Julia Ward, editor. **Sex and Education.** 1874.

La Follette, Suzanne. **Concerning Women.** 1926.

Leslie, Eliza. **Miss Leslie's Behaviour Book: A Guide and Manual for Ladies.** 1859.

Livermore, Mary A. **My Story of the War.** 1889.

Logan, Mrs. John A. (Mary S.) **The Part Taken By Women in American History.** 1912.

McGuire, Judith W. (A Lady of Virginia). **Diary of a Southern Refugee, During the War.** 1867.

Mann, Herman. **The Female Review: Life of Deborah Sampson.** 1866.

Meyer, Annie Nathan, editor. **Woman's Work in America.** 1891.

Myerson, Abraham. **The Nervous Housewife.** 1927.

Parsons, Elsie Clews. **The Old-Fashioned Woman.** 1913.

Porter, Sarah Harvey. **The Life and Times of Anne Royall.** 1909.

Pruette, Lorine. **Women and Leisure: A Study of Social Waste.** 1924.

Salmon, Lucy Maynard. **Domestic Service.** 1897.

Sanger, William W. **The History of Prostitution.** 1859.

Smith, Julia E. **Abby Smith and Her Cows.** 1877.

Spencer, Anna Garlin. **Woman's Share in Social Culture.** 1913.

Sprague, William Forrest. **Women and the West.** 1940.

Stanton, Elizabeth Cady. **The Woman's Bible** Parts I and II. 1895/1898.

Stewart, Mrs. Eliza Daniel. **Memories of the Crusade.** 1889.

Todd, John. **Woman's Rights.** 1867. [Dodge, Mary A.] (Gail Hamilton, pseud.) **Woman's Wrongs.** 1868.

Van Rensselaer, Mrs. John King. **The Goede Vrouw of Mana-ha-ta.** 1898.

Velazquez, Loreta Janeta. **The Woman in Battle.** 1876.

Vietor, Agnes C., editor. **A Woman's Quest: The Life of Marie E. Zakrzewska, M.D.** 1924.

Woodbury, Helen L. Sumner. **Equal Suffrage.** 1909.

Young, Ann Eliza. **Wife No. 19.** 1875.